S0-BBG-214

# NEEDLEPOINT LETTERS AND NUMBERS

# NEEDLEPOINT LETTERS AND NUMBERS

by
Carol Cheney Rome
and
Donna Reidy Orr

Doubleday & Company, Inc.
Garden City, New York 1977

**To Anne Middleton Jones and Wm. Reed Orr**

Frontis: Roman Magesty "D"

Library of Congress Cataloging in Publication Data

Rome, Carol Cheney.
Needlepoint letters and numbers.

Bibliography: p. 159.
Includes index.
1. Canvas embroidery—Patterns. 2. Alphabets.
3. Numerals. I. Orr, Donna Reidy, joint author.
II. Title.
TT778.C3R63 746.4'4
ISBN 0-385-09980-0
Library of Congress Catalog Card Number 73-36609

Printed in the United States of America
First Edition

# CONTENTS

# ACKNOWLEDGMENTS

Many people have helped us in the preparation of this book. We wish to thank Rabbi Erwin M. Halpern, Congregation Beth Am, Houston, for his advice on the Hebrew sayings. Jean Mailey, of the Metropolitan Museum of Art, New York, helped us with sources for stitched alphabets, including the Chinese Terrestrial Signs. Susan Newman has taken care of all our business, and Karen Van Westering, our editor at Doubleday, worked hard to untangle the technical kinks that invariably accompany a book of this nature. Iva Roddey and Cynthia Langhorne have been invaluable to us; they did much of the rendered artwork and gave their advice on some of the alphabets prone to inconsistency. Tom Menefee printed our black-and-white pictures, and we thank him for prompt and excellent work in the darkroom.

Many friends and associates helped launch the book by lending their time in stitching the alphabets and many of the projects shown in color. Without them, there would not have been enough hours to get the job done; Lillian Shetler, who never lost her temper and who loaned her house as well as her time, Georgianna Verbrugge, Verna Holme, Sally Boom, Dot Sandlin, Nancy Hoffman, Ann Dean, LeAnne Orr, Mary Nall, Jeane Aston, and Jodee Schmalhausen. Our families have displayed super sportsmanship and haven't complained about our time spent away from them, for which we are extremely grateful.

*Carol Cheney Rome and Donna Reidy Orr*

# LETTERING IN EMBROIDERY

"All writing in its early history was a sacred and mysterious form of expression . . . the letter was the symbol . . . and was adorned just as carefully as the altar itself." So explains Alexander Nesbitt in his forward to *Decorative Alphabets and Initials*. The devotion of early scribes to their labor on religious works, such as the Irish Book of Kells and the Lindisfarne Gospels, was matched by those whose work was to stitch altar vestments and priestly robes. In fact, the embroiderer was often aided by draftsmen and painters in designing the ecclesiástical work that enriched the house of worship.

Aside from church-related subject matter, lettering came to be used in embroidery in such interesting pieces as the Bayeux Tapestry, a two-hundred-foot-long embroidery in comic strip fashion, that depicts the Norman version of events leading to William the Conqueror's victory over the Anglo-Saxon Army in 1066. The work was done within twelve years after the Battle of Hastings, and words were used to help explain the various scenes that run the length of the embroidery.

Although lettering remained an important part of ecclesiastical embroidery through the ages, the dawn of heraldry gave another impetus to the stitcher to add lettering to embroidery. Family crests and coats of arms were embroidered on highly prized household linens, and monograms and ciphers were added to fancy work done in the royal houses. Later, samplers were worked by young women for practice in stitching borders and letters. Styles of embroidered letters reflected the handwritten and later the type-set alphabets that were in vogue at the time. During the Victorian era, there was an explosion of lettering styles, many quite ornate and bizarre in design. During this time, too, all sorts of plain and fancy needlework were done by all of womankind. The surge of interest in new and different alphabets was met with monthly publications of charted letters by Godey's, among other publishers.

While much of the Victoriana is "beyond help" for the stitcher of today, we can still find many samples from the last century that are both attractive and likely candidates for use in needlepoint. Added to that are the Gothic and classical Roman styles and the alphabets generated in our own era, and there is certainly more than enough to choose from.

It is hoped that you will find several alphabet styles in this book to use in your needlepoint. If you wish to go beyond this, there is some instruction at the back of the book on working out your own alphabets.

This sampler by Julia Ann Niver, dated 1833, is typical of the work done by countless school girls in the 1800s. The gauge of the grounding fabric is quite tiny, and there is a combination of Cross Stitch and other counted thread stitches, as well as some that we tend to associate with needlepoint. Note the zigzag border, worked in Rococo, that separates the various alphabets from the biblical verse and scene. Courtesy of the Cooper-Hewitt Museum of Decorative Arts and Design, Smithsonian Institution.

Dymphna Ellis, who worked her sampler "in the last year of the Great War" was a very skillful stitcher. The sampler is attractively laid out, with various counted thread stitches forming border motifs, the alphabets, and the religious verse. Adam and Eve are at the top with two dogs, two stags, and two bees. Two of the alphabets in this sampler served as inspiration for ones that are diagramed in this book, Early Sampler (page 60) and Victorian Eyelet (page 49). The collection of Cora Ginsburg, Tarrytown, New York.

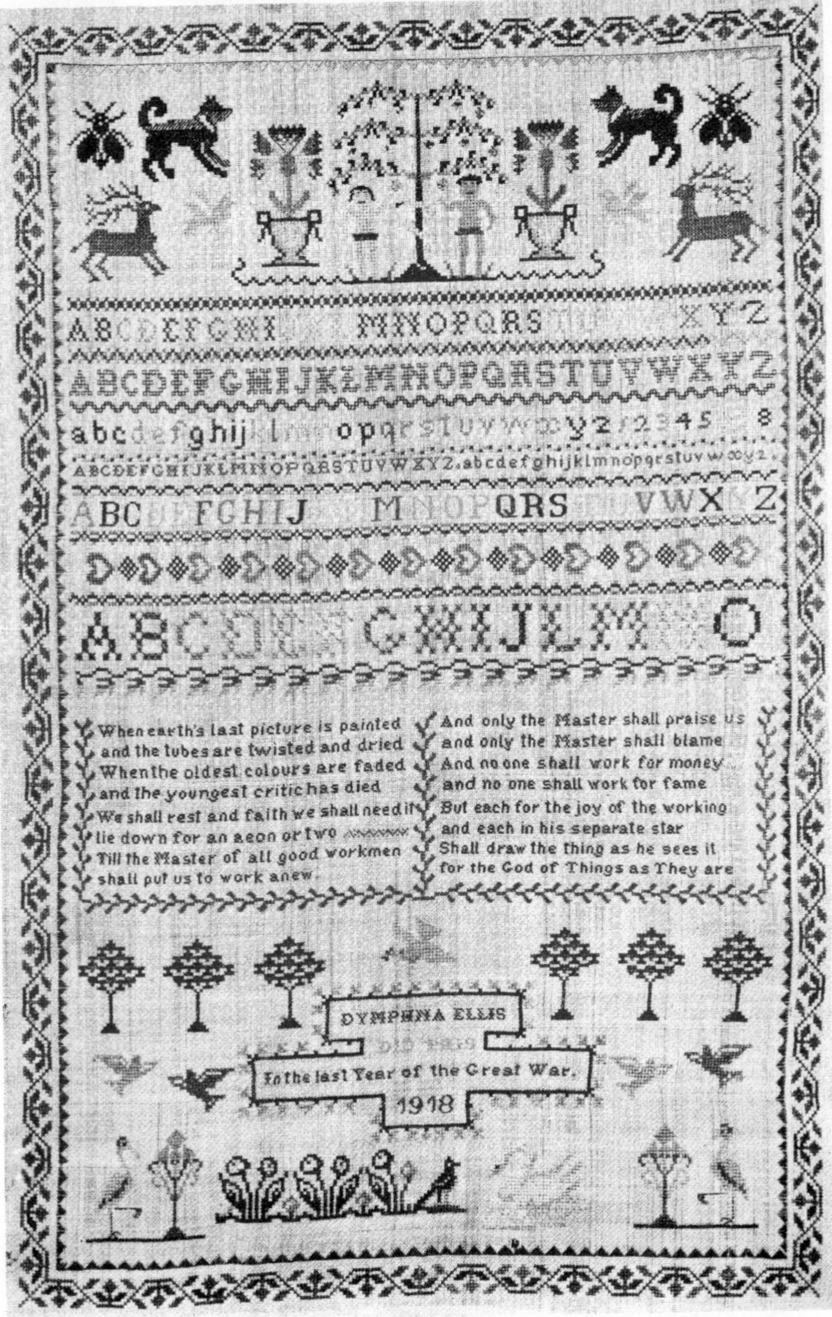

# HOW TO USE THIS BOOK

The alphabets and numbers in this book are graphed just as you would stitch them, with no mental gymnastics necessary to decode complicated charts and instructions. A variety of styles is presented; for each, the heights of the letters and the number of strands of Persian yarn needed to stitch them on 14-ct. canvas (14 threads to the square inch) are given. The true center of each letter, as placed in "an invisible block," is marked with a circle as a further convenience to stitching the alphabets.

*Note to the forgotten minority:* Careful attention is paid to the left-handed stitcher in this book, with diagrams reworked or special instructions given where necessary. It is high time that you receive individual attention.

After deciding where you want to use a letter(s), and choosing an appropriate alphabet style for the project at hand, some careful counting is necessary to get things set up right.

1. Count the number of threads in the area where the letter will be situated; be sure to count canvas threads, NOT holes.
2. Divide the length and width in half and mark on the mid-lines. You can use a hard No. 3 pencil, a pretested, colorfast marker in a pale color, or use a running stitch with sewing thread. Counting canvas threads is made easier if you keep this analogy in mind. Pretend you are working with railroad tracks. Put your pencil point in a hole and listen for the "click" as the pencil passes over each thread, or each rail tie, and draw the lines on between the tracks. Where the mid-lines intersect, as shown in the photograph, is the center of the area.
3. If you only count the number of letters in the word(s) you want to stitch, your design may be thrown off center. The number of threads on one line to be covered with a monogram or word(s), *plus* the space threads in between the letters must be added together. Divide this total number in half to find the true center of your design, which may fall within a letter or between letters. Count from right to left.
4. Regardless of the width of the letter (whether it is an odd or even number of canvas threads wide), right-handed stitchers will bring the needle up at the canvas center and start stitching the letter to the left and down. Note the circled center of each letter to help you get started. If the center does not actually fall on the letter itself, start stitching as close to the true center as possible. Left-handed stitchers should bring the needle to the front of the canvas, up one, and across to the right one thread from the penciled center. You will start working the letter to the right and up.
5. You will have to use a combination of Tent stitches to finish the letter. Because of this, the usual method of "swinging" the needle (sewing from the surface side of the canvas) is not very satisfactory when working on letters. Canvas distortion and lumpy-looking stitches can be minimized if you "push and poke" the letter stitches and the background stitches immediately surrounding each letter. It is not objectionable to skip around a bit without ending a thread, but make sure the yarn on the canvas back is couched down later with background stitching and that very dark threads do not run under pale background colors.

The spacing between letters is as important as the letters themselves. It is preferable to pack the letters together, leaving fewer threads between them than you would first guess. The space between words should be equivalent to a wide capital letter, such as "O." Also, do not leave too many threads between lines of letters, or the design will look scattered. Time and tears can be saved by working out words on graph paper before stitching.

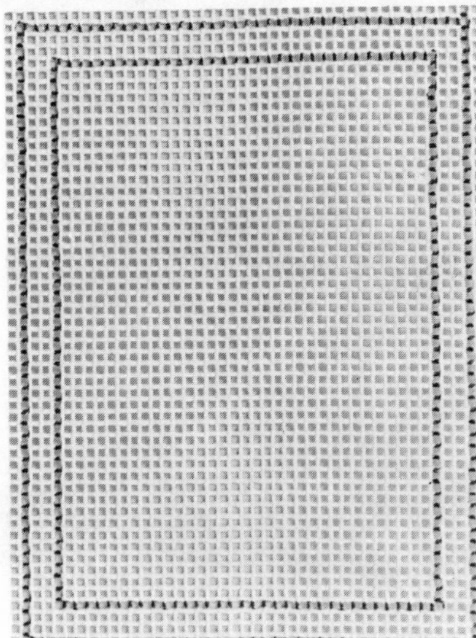

Marked off canvas area that will contain a letter.

The mid-lines of the rectangle are counted and marked to establish the center.

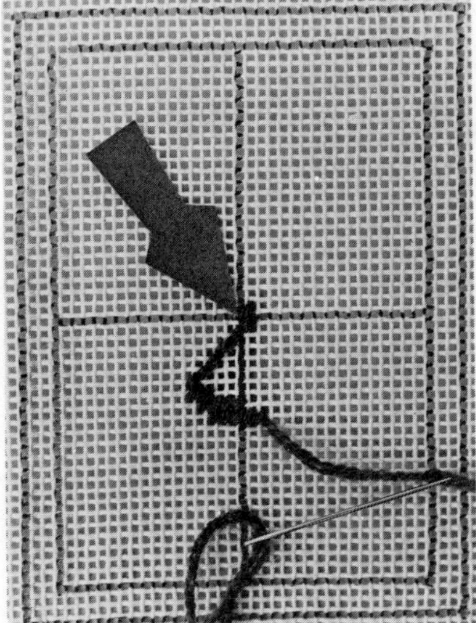

Following the diagram for an upper case Gothic "C" (page 45), the needle is brought up in the center of the canvas, and the stitching is started at the center of the letter to the left and then down. The centers of letters are marked on the diagrams in this book with small circles.

The letter is completed, and now the background and border can be stitched in around it.

Two letters appear in the panel. The center of the rectangle is established, and then the letters are positioned to right and left of this point. Note that the letters have fewer threads between them than are at the sides, but the effect is very well-balanced. Note: When working with more than one letter, the width of all letters and space in between must be added together and then divided in half to center the letters as a unit within the background panel. The letters are Contemporary Stripe (page 39) with Backstitches worked down the middle of the Stem fillers. The purse is a premounted denim piece.

Three Monogram Block (page 24) letters are centered to make up the monogram. The middle large "O" is centered in the middle of the space allotted for letters, and the small "L" and "A" are positioned using the "O" as a guide. Note that the letters actually touch, but the monogram does not look crowded. The background around the monogram is Stem stitch shaded by mixing different colors together and stitching with them at the same time. This is a close-up of the jewelry box that appears in color on page vi.

The Script (page 32) name block shows several letters combined to form first and last name. The spacing of these letters happens to come to 2 threads with a wider space left between words. However, no mathematical formula can be followed for spacing, and it is important to graph out words and sentences to get attractive layouts. What looks right is right.

## TENT—THE STAPLE STITCH

The Tent stitch (alias Continental, Half Cross, Petit Point, Gros Point, Diagonal Tent, and Basketweave) always looks the same on the front of the canvas, slanting from lower left to upper right over one canvas intersection. The stitch can be worked in horizontal, vertical or diagonal rows. Once you master the Tent stitch, you will have gone a long way in perfecting your needlepoint "penmanship."

The Tent stitch worked horizontally or vertically is often called Continental. This is a.o.k. for filling in a thin letter or for outlining a fat one, but it tends to distort the canvas and should be restricted to one or two rows. When working across, right-handed stitchers should work from right to left starting at the top. Left-handed stitchers should begin at the bottom and work from left to right. The canvas can be turned upside down to begin each new row.

Continental worked vertically should also be restricted to one or two rows. Right-handed stitchers work from top to bottom, starting at the right, while left-handed stitchers work from bottom to top, starting at the left. The canvas can be rotated to start new rows.

Basketweave, the king of Tent stitches, is worked diagonally and forms a sturdy woven backing that does not warp the canvas nearly as much as the horizontal and vertical methods. The tricks to working perfect, painless Basketweave are shown visually in the composite diagrams. (Left-handed stitchers: By now you can see why you will start your center letter stitch above and to the right of the marked canvas center.) One more hint to help you with Basketweave—when beginning and ending threads, run them vertically or horizontally under stitching on the back, disturbing the basket pattern as little as possible. Keep the tail ends clipped very close so they won't pop through later while you're working the background.

A word about backgrounds. You will find that many of the bold, big stitches you may have learned in a sampler class are not suitable for filling in the interstices of letters. Try to choose a small stitch for the background if you aren't going to use Basketweave. Save the other stitches for borders and embellishments outside the lettering area or you will spend a lot of time making compensating stitches that look ragged and unattractive.

Alphabets using stitches other than Tent—or in combination with Tent—are diagramed in complete detail to help you get started. And now, on to happy lettering.

## CONTINENTAL WORKED HORIZONTALLY

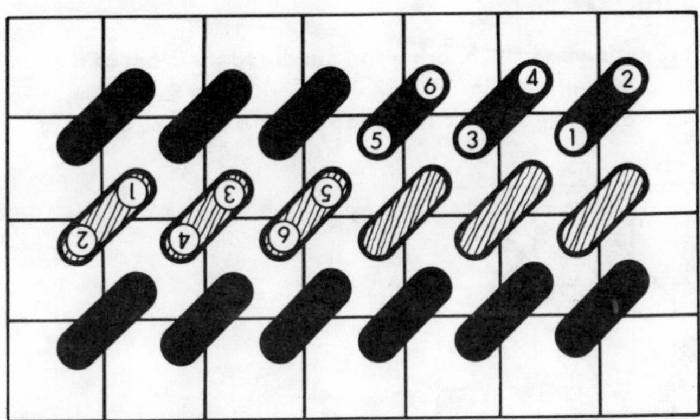


RIGHT-HANDED STITCHERS

Horizontal Tent (Continental) stitch. Bring the needle to the front of the canvas at 1 and take it to the back at 2. Work from right to left, turning the canvas upside down (rotating the canvas) at the ends of rows and starting each new row at the right side.

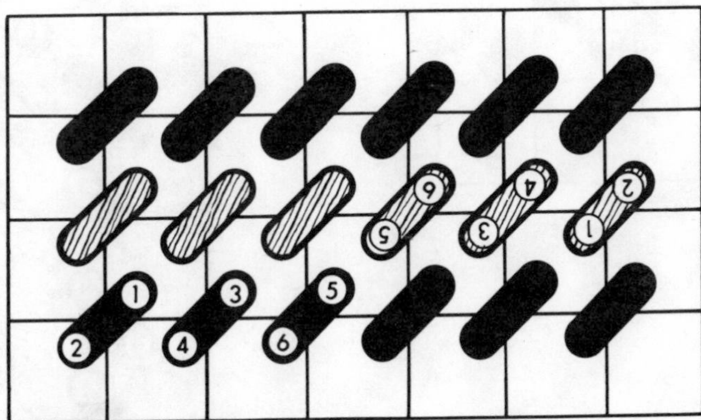


LEFT-HANDED STITCHERS

Horizontal Tent (Continental) stitch. Bring the needle to the front of the canvas at 1 and take it to the back at 2. Work from left to right, turning the canvas upside down (rotating the canvas) at the ends of rows and starting each new row at the left side.

## CONTINENTAL WORKED VERTICALLY

RIGHT-HANDED STITCHERS

Vertical Tent (Continental) stitch. Bring the needle to the front of the canvas at 1 and take it to the back at 2. Work from top to bottom, rotating the canvas at the ends of rows and starting each new row at the top.

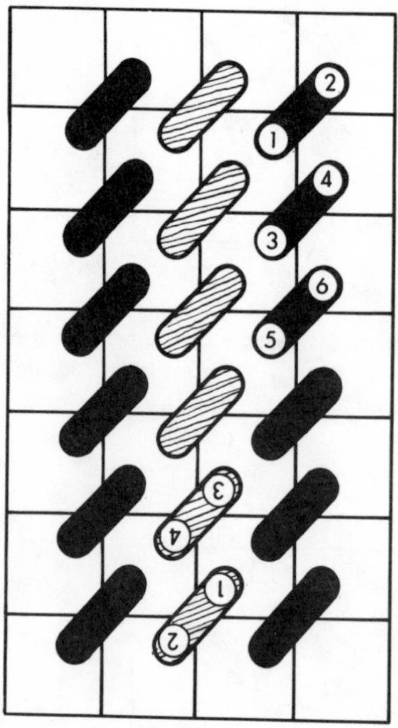


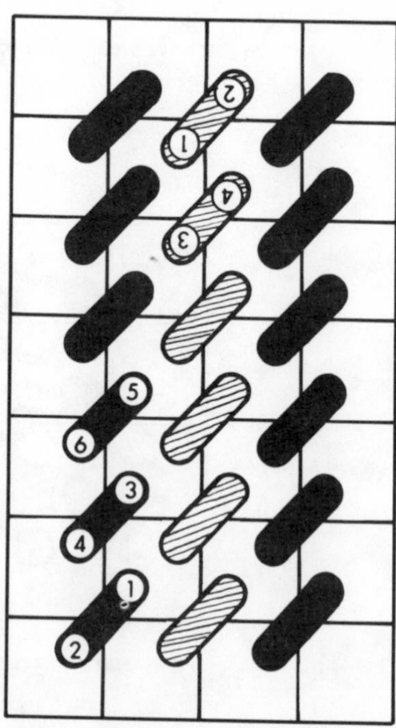


LEFT-HANDED STITCHERS

Vertical Tent (Continental) stitch. Bring the needle to the front of the canvas at 1 and take it to the back at 2. Work from bottom to top, rotating the canvas at the ends of rows and starting each new row at the bottom.

## BASKETWEAVE

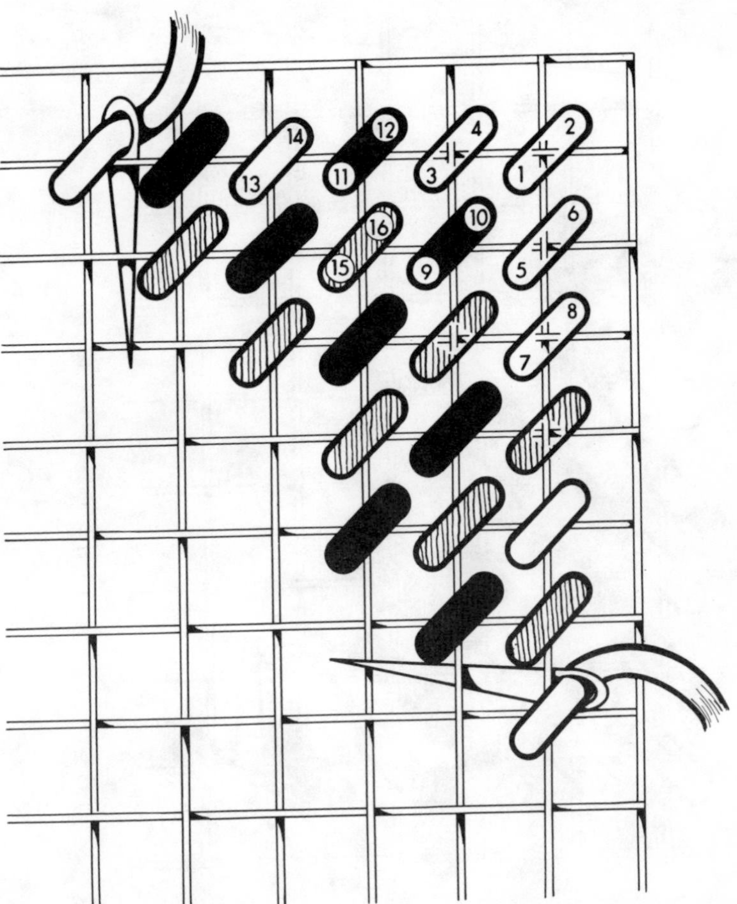


RIGHT-HANDED STITCHERS

Basketweave. Bring the needle to the front of the canvas at 1 and take it to the back at 2. The stitches at the top and side left open indicate the turning, or compensating, stitch necessary to start a new row. The black stitches show "up" rows, and the striped stitches show "down" rows. You will notice that the needle swings straight across to the left under 2 canvas threads to each new stitch in "up" rows. The needle swings straight down under 2 canvas threads to each new stitch in "down" rows. Further, you will notice that a horizontal canvas thread is on top of the intersection when an "up" row is stitched. A vertical thread is on top when a "down" row is stitched. The needle position is parallel to the canvas thread on top, to help you remember.

## BASKETWEAVE

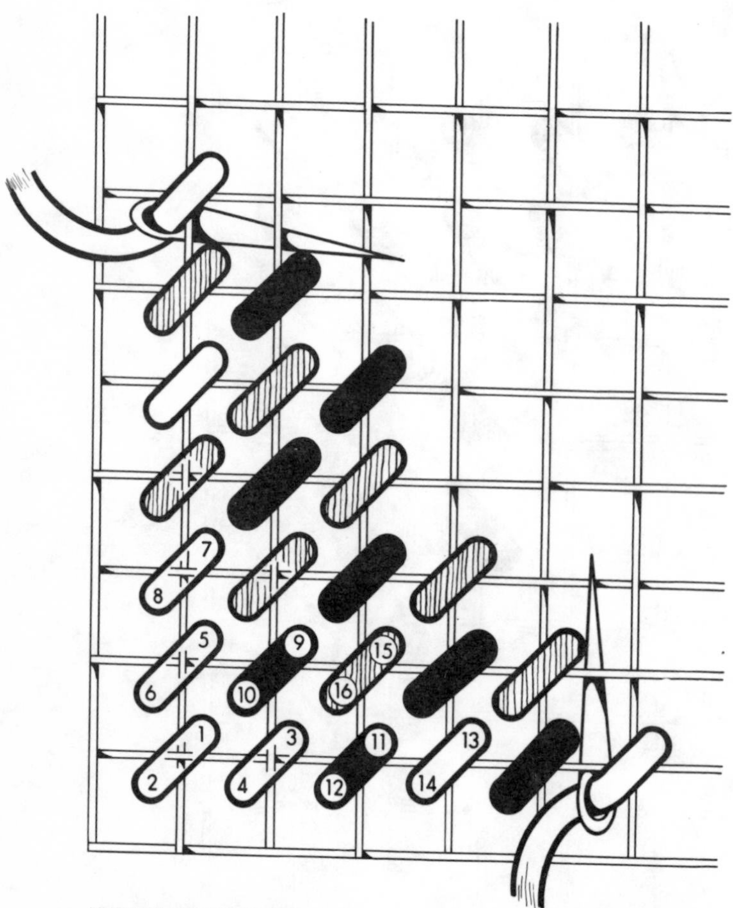


LEFT-HANDED STITCHERS

Basketweave. Bring the needle to the front of the canvas at 1 and take it to the back at 2. The stitches at the bottom and side left open indicate the turning, or compensating, stitch necessary to start a new row. The black stitches show "down" rows, and the striped stitches show "up" rows. You will notice that the needle swings straight across to the right under 2 canvas threads to each new stitch in "down" rows. The needle swings straight up under 2 canvas threads to each new stitch in "up" rows. Further, you will notice that a vertical canvas thread is on top of the intersection when an "up" row is stitched. A horizontal thread is on top when a "down" row is stitched. The needle position is parallel to the canvas thread on top, to help you remember.

# THE ALPHABETS

# SLIM LINE

**Double strand on 14-ct. canvas**
**height: large letters – 14 threads**
**small letters – 9 threads**

The Slim Line letters are very useful in small, upright rectangular areas. Both sizes can be combined in monograms, with the last initial placed in the middle in the 14-thread height, flanked by two 9-thread letters.

A color picture using Slim Line appears on page viii.

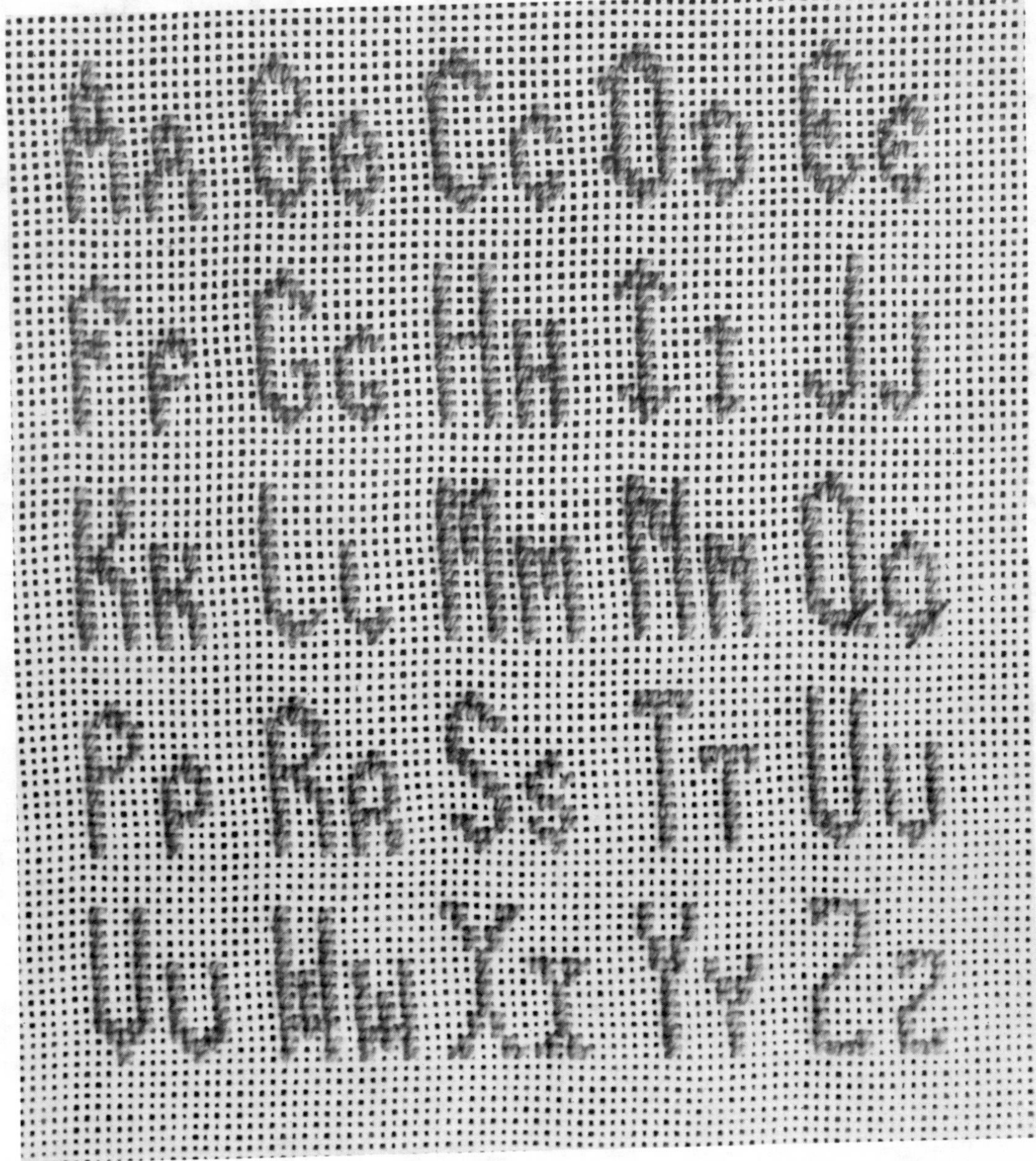

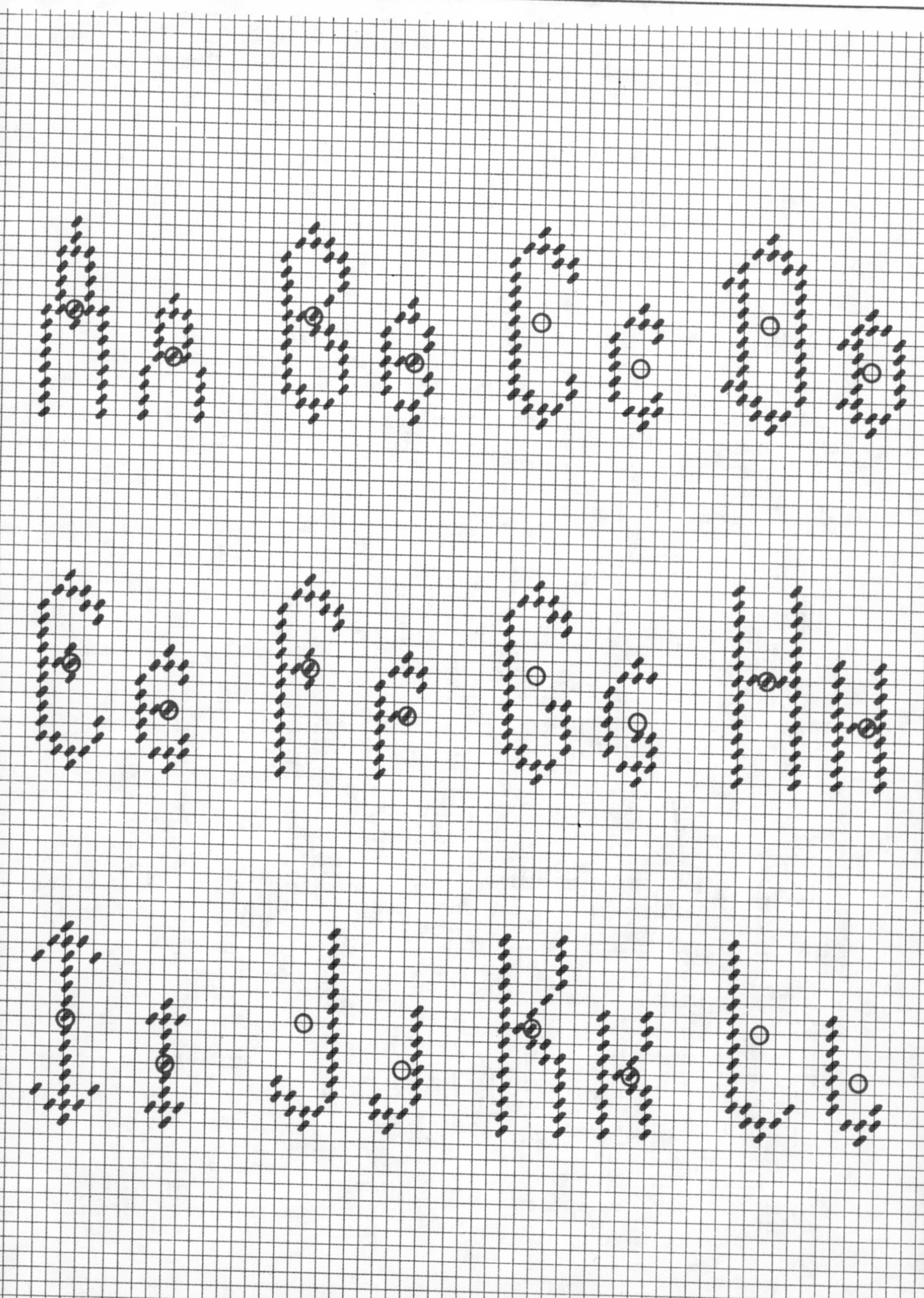

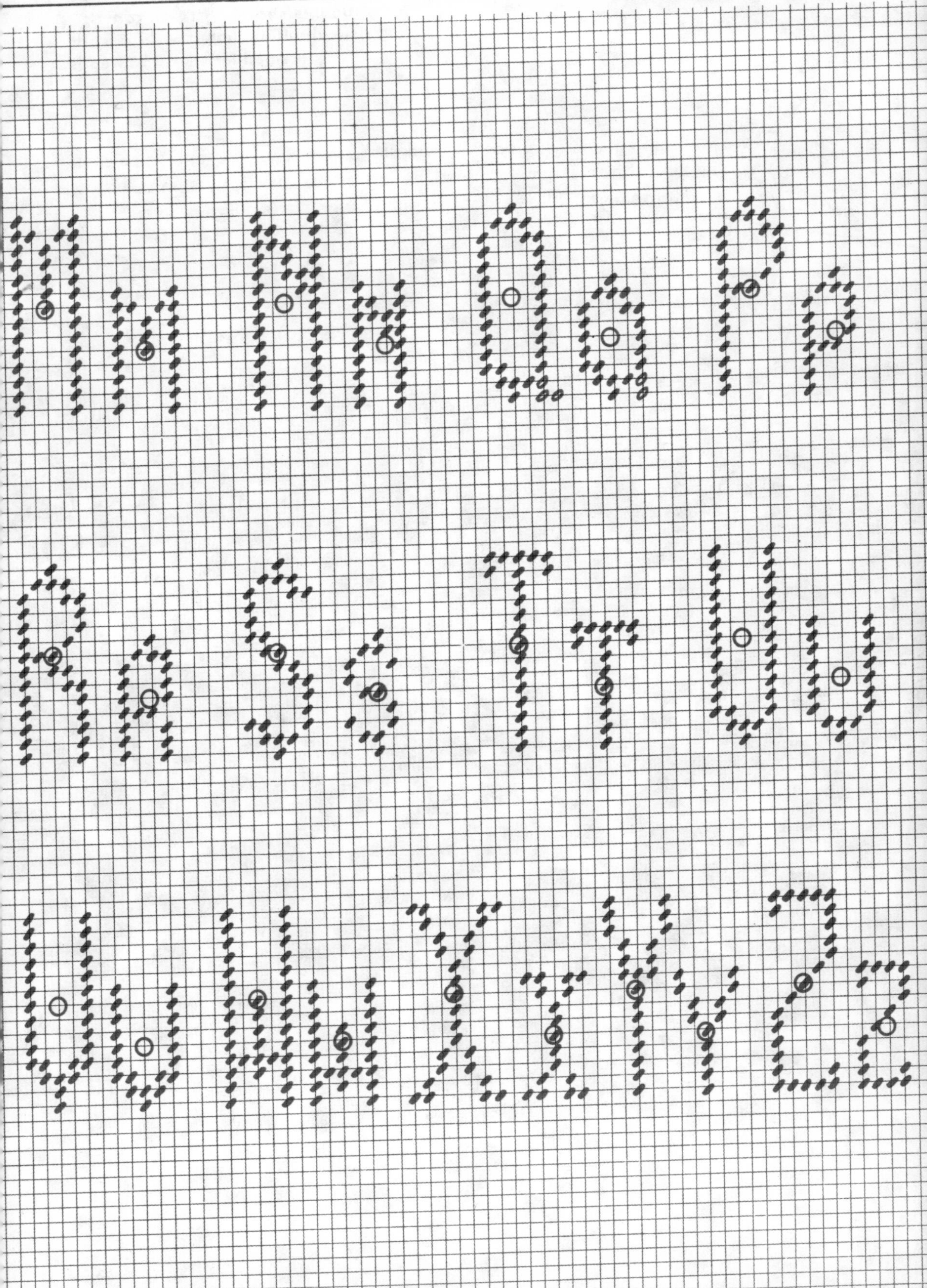

# MONOGRAM BLOCKS

**Double strand on 14-ct. canvas**
**height: large letters – 25 threads**
**small letters – 15 threads**

These versatile letters are easiest to work if the outline of the letter is stitched first to get the correct count, and then the rest of the letter is filled in with Basketweave. Large and small sizes look attractive together in a monogram.

A color picture of Monogram Blocks is shown on page vi.

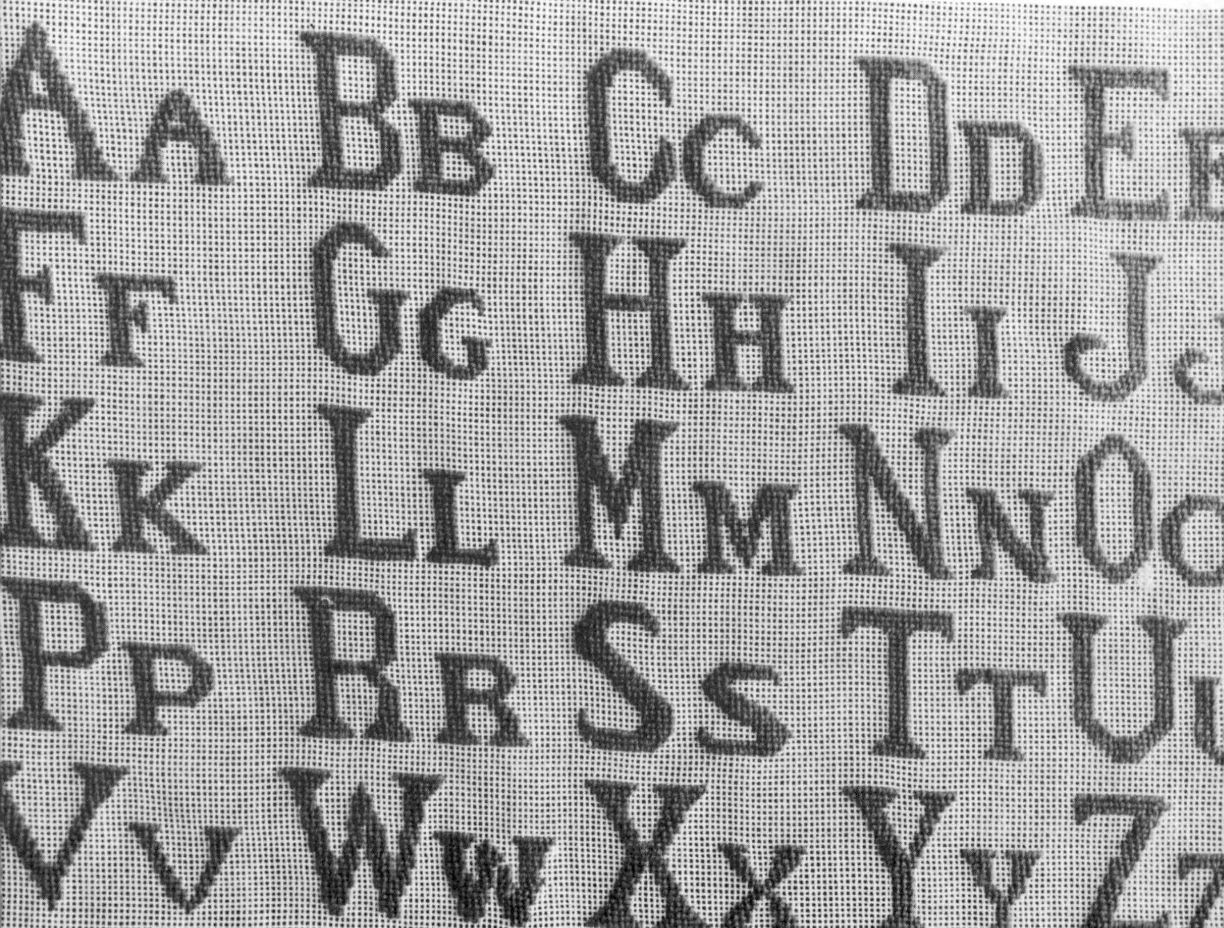

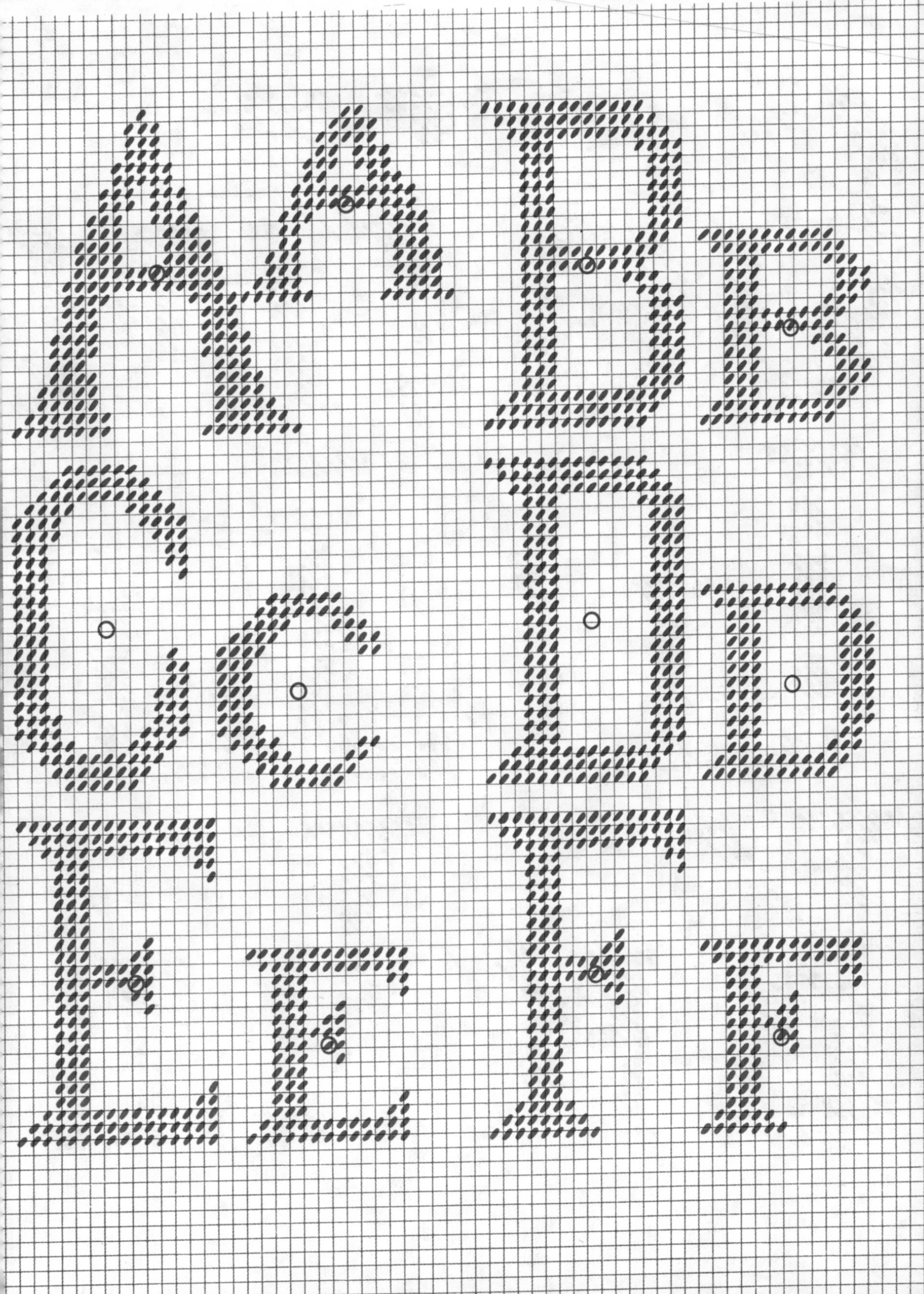

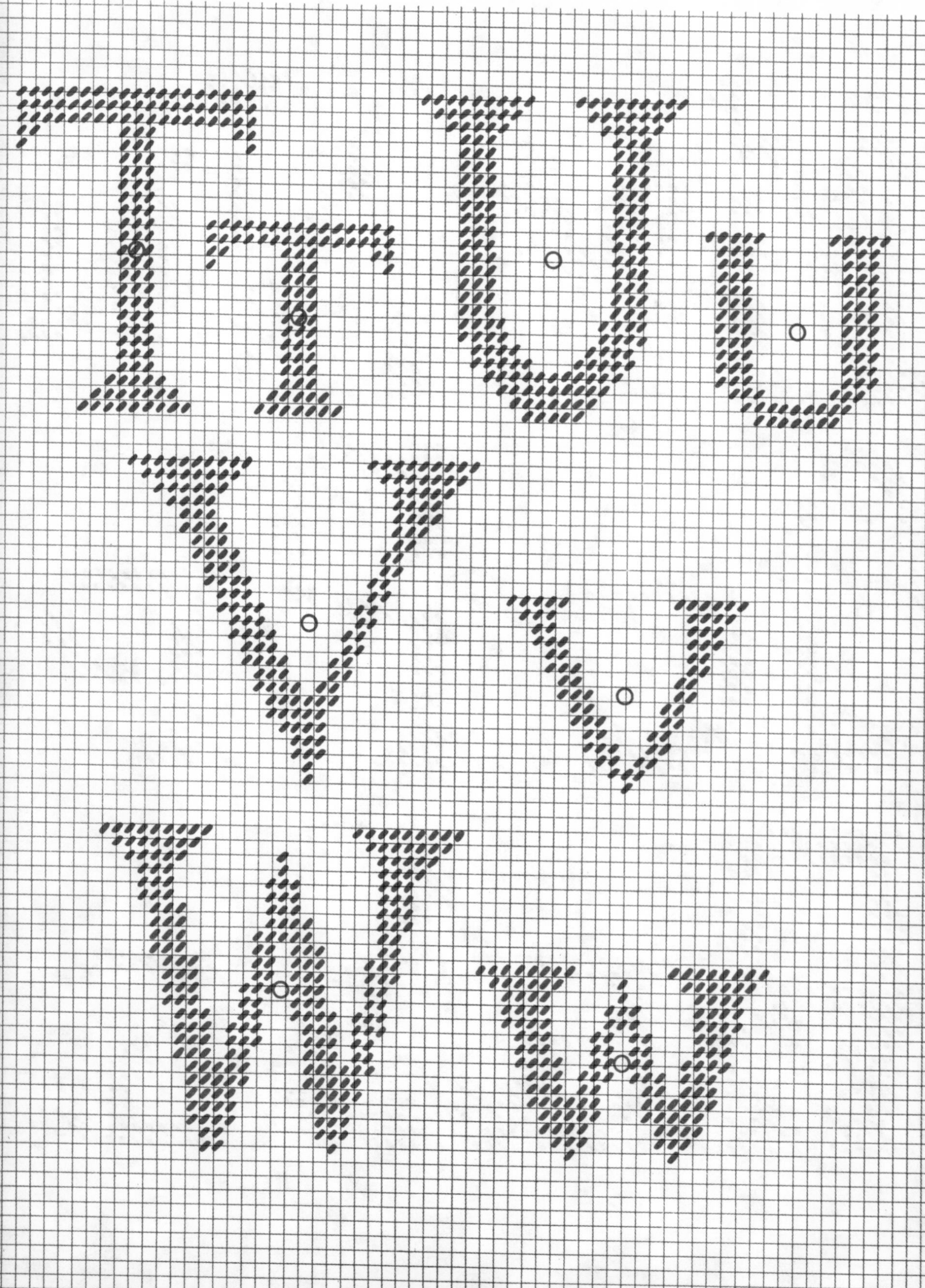

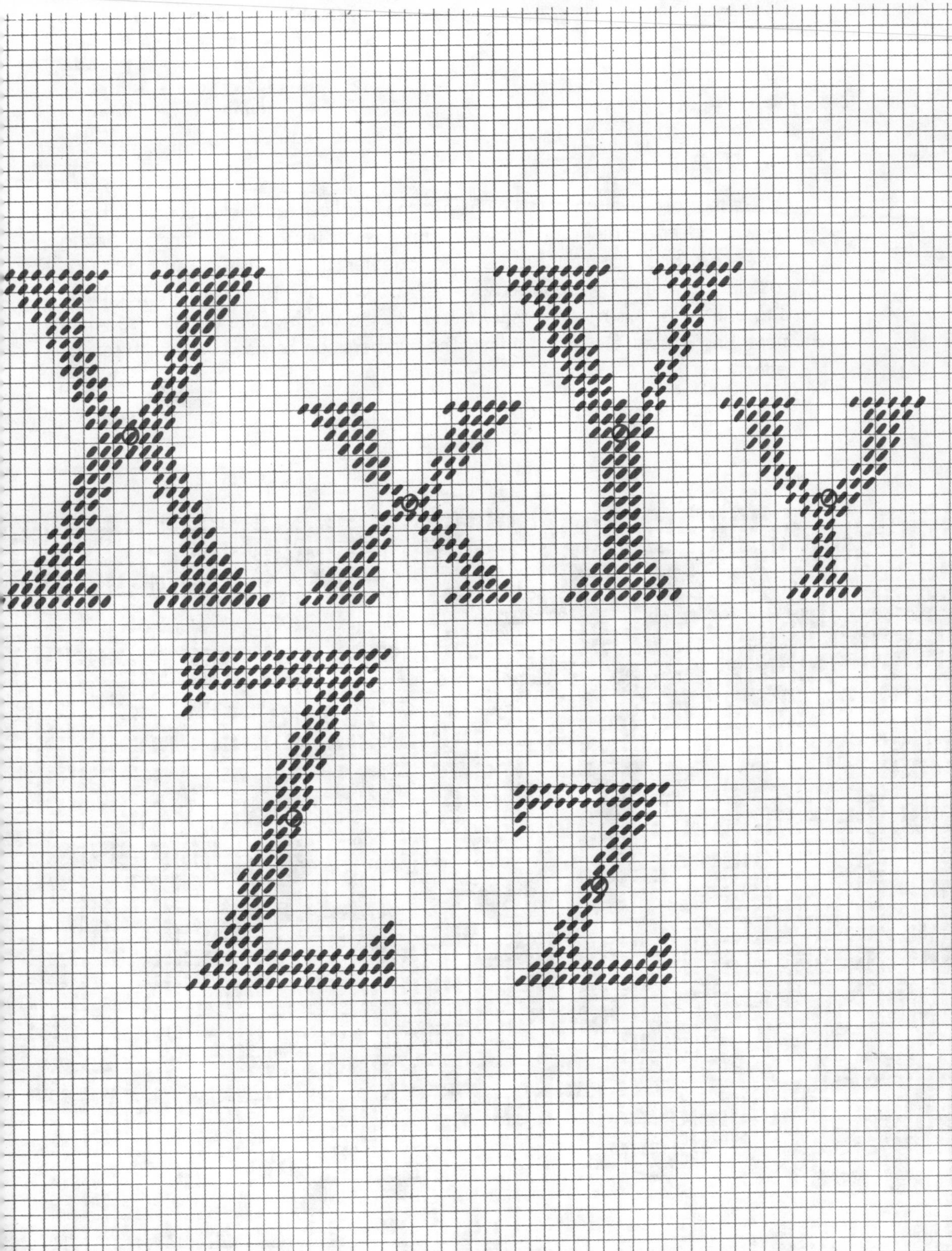

# LILLIPUTIAN

**Double strand on 14-ct. canvas**
**height: upper case – 5 threads**
**numbers – 5 threads**
**lower case – 5 threads**
**numbers – 5 threads**

Letters that are 5 threads in height are the smallest readable letters that can be worked in needlepoint. Presented here is an upper-case alphabet and a lower-case one, not meant to be used together. If you wish to use the lower-case letters with a few upper-case ones, you will have to add to the height by 3 to 5 threads. It is not necessary to add to the width of the upper case when increasing its size. Do graph it first. The numbers can be used with both sets of letters.

A color picture using Lilliputian appears on page ii.

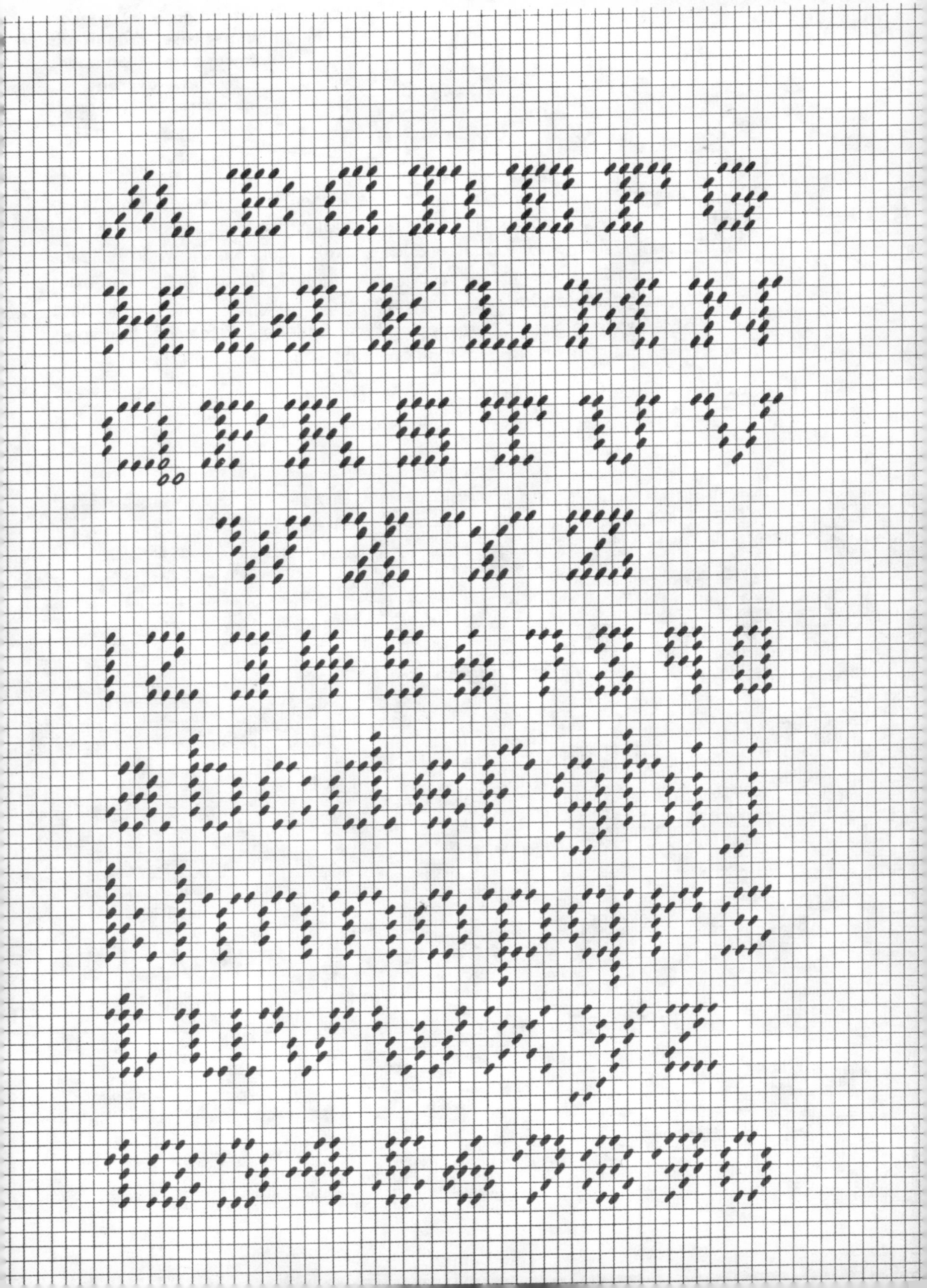

# SCRIPT

**Double strand on 14-ct. canvas**
**height: upper case – 16 threads**
**lower case – 6 threads**
**base average**
**numbers – 12 threads**

The combination of upper- and lower-case letters here gives you an opportunity to make word groups for names and quotations or slogans. The style of the alphabet is somewhat formal. The lower-case letters are shown in sentence form to demonstrate how the letters connect together. Usually there is an extra stitch on either side of the letter. However, we recommend that you graph a word or sentence to get the best spacing between letters. Remember that spacing is based more on eye appeal than on math.

Color pictures of projects using Script are on pages v and viii.

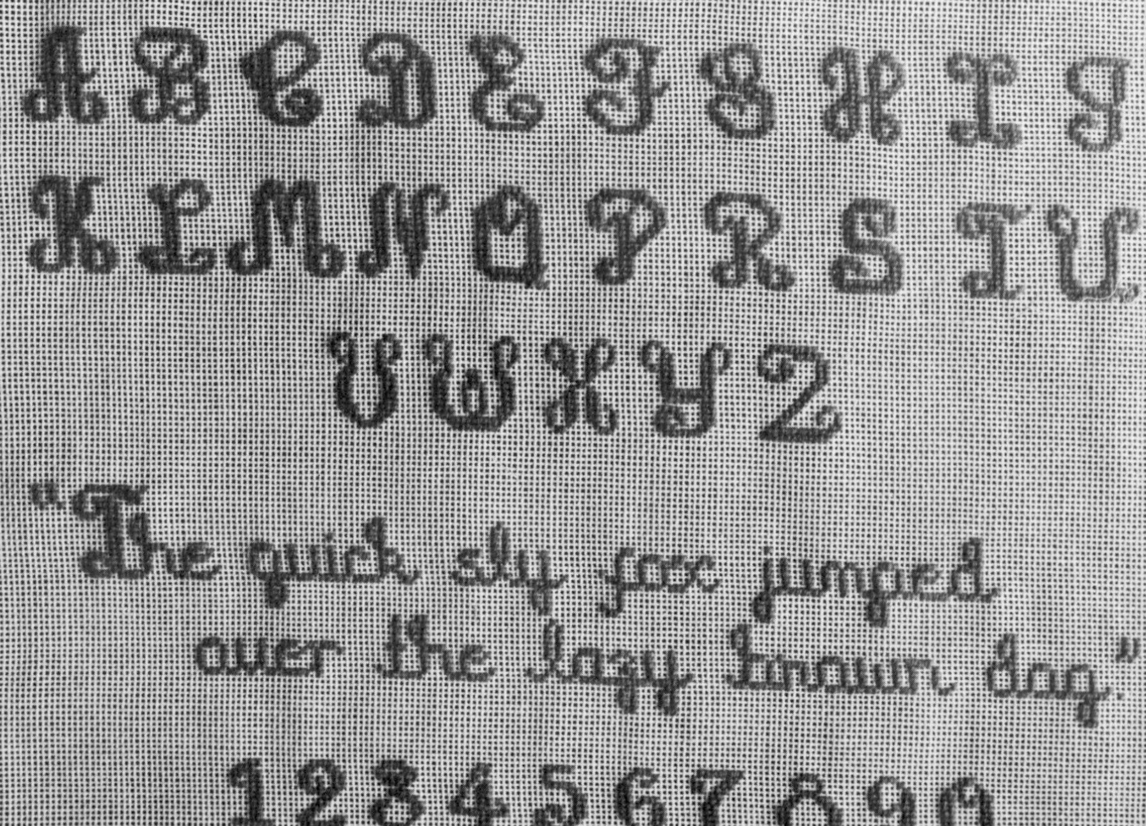

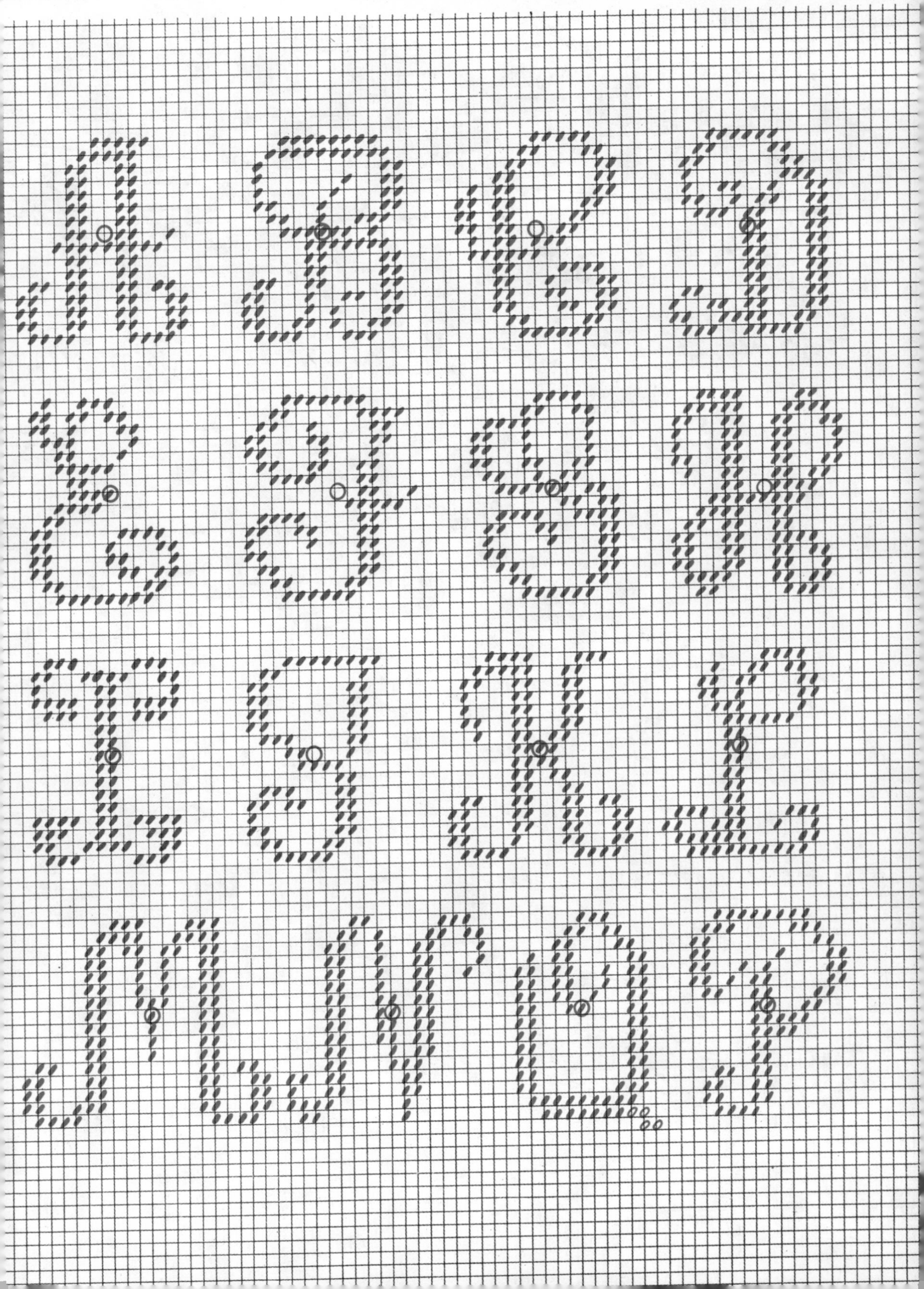

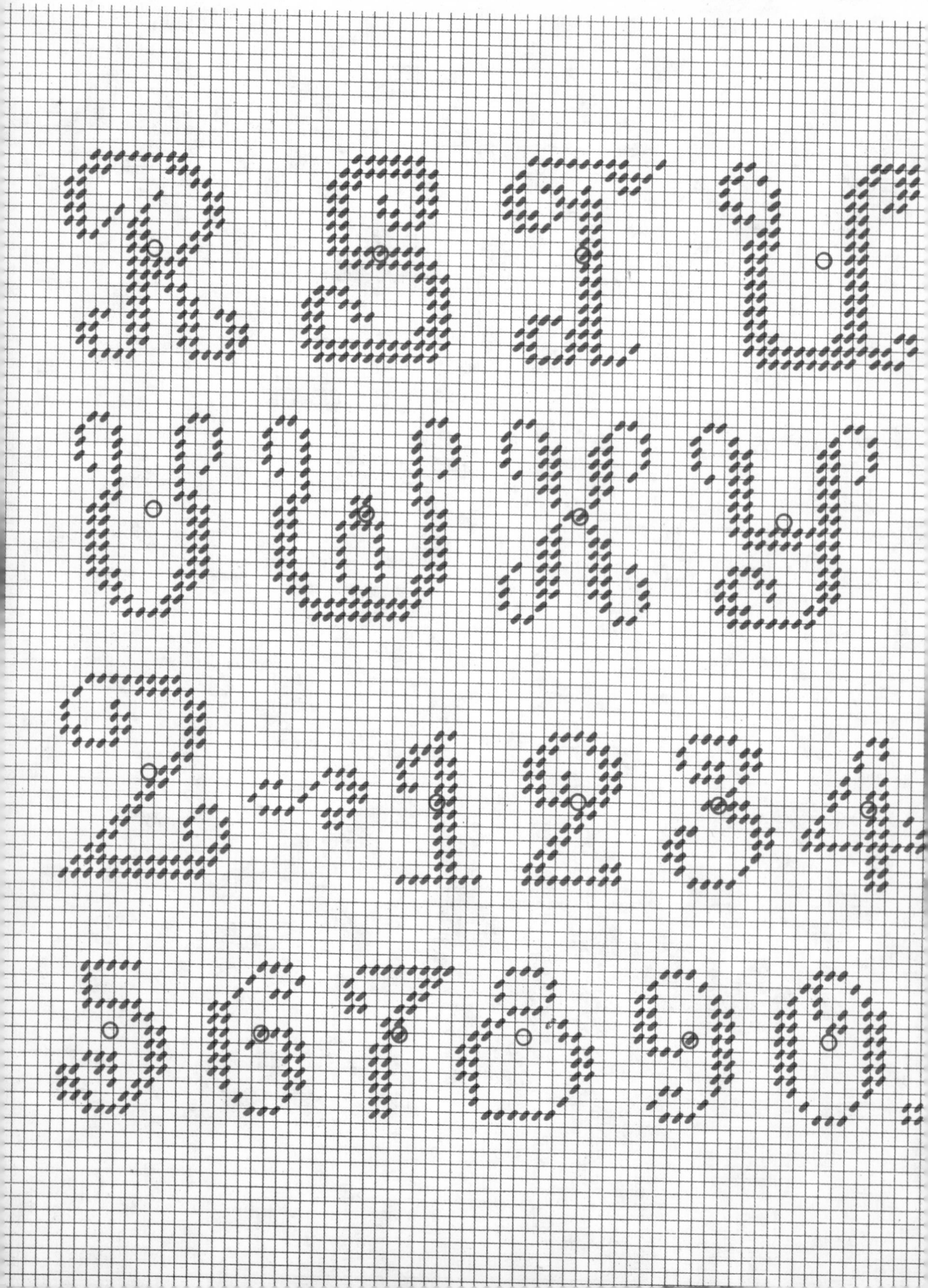

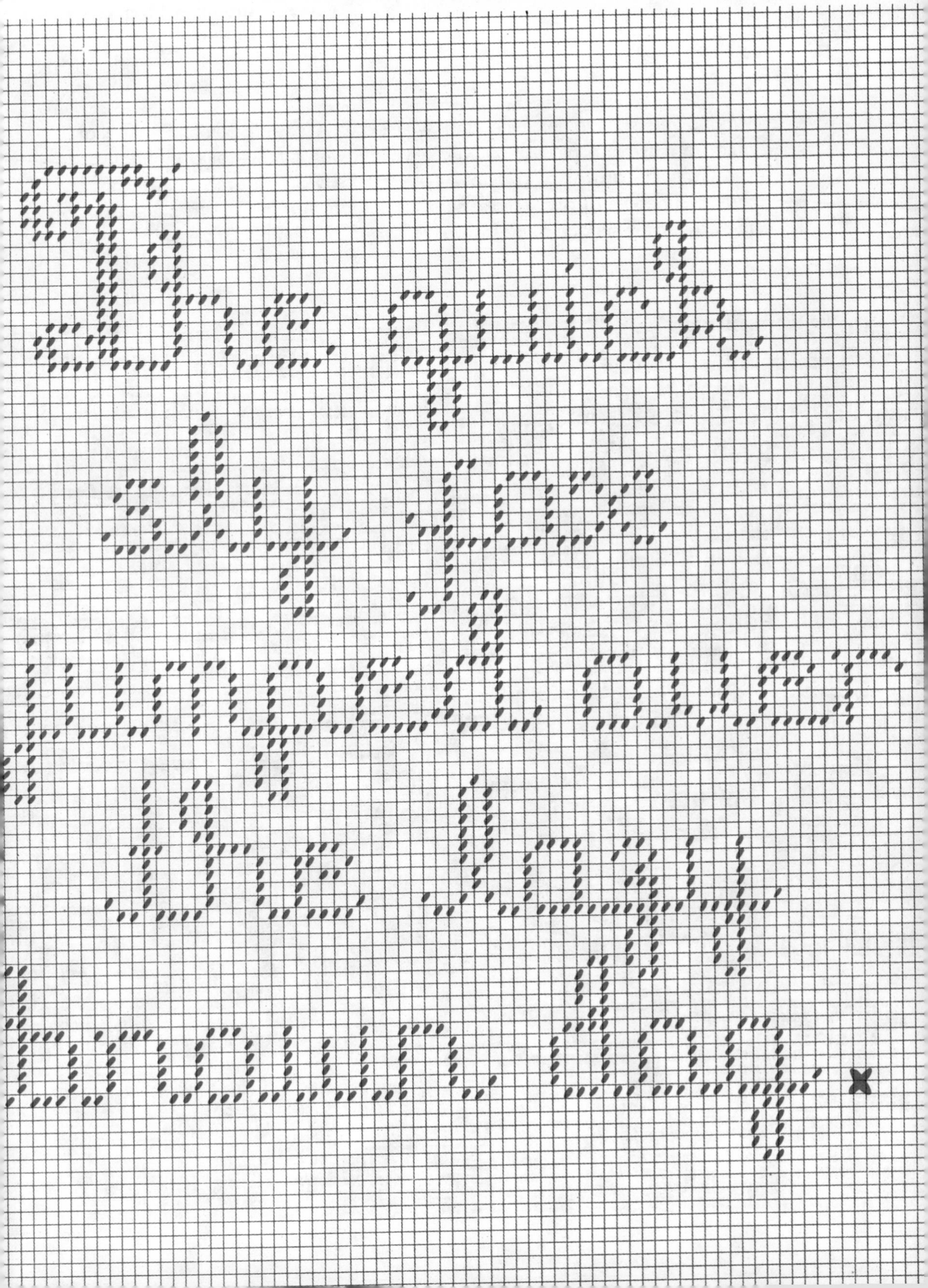
The quick
sly fox
jumped over
the lazy
brown dog

# WILD FLOWER

**Double strand on 14-ct. canvas**
**height: 16 threads**

Wildflower is quite feminine and whimsical. A sweet, personal gift that is quick to make is a pincushion with a Wildflower initial—for a birthday or to celebrate the arrival of a baby. You will be working with more than one threaded needle at once; make sure the threads not in use are pinned out of the way on the surface of the canvas to avoid creating a "rat's nest."

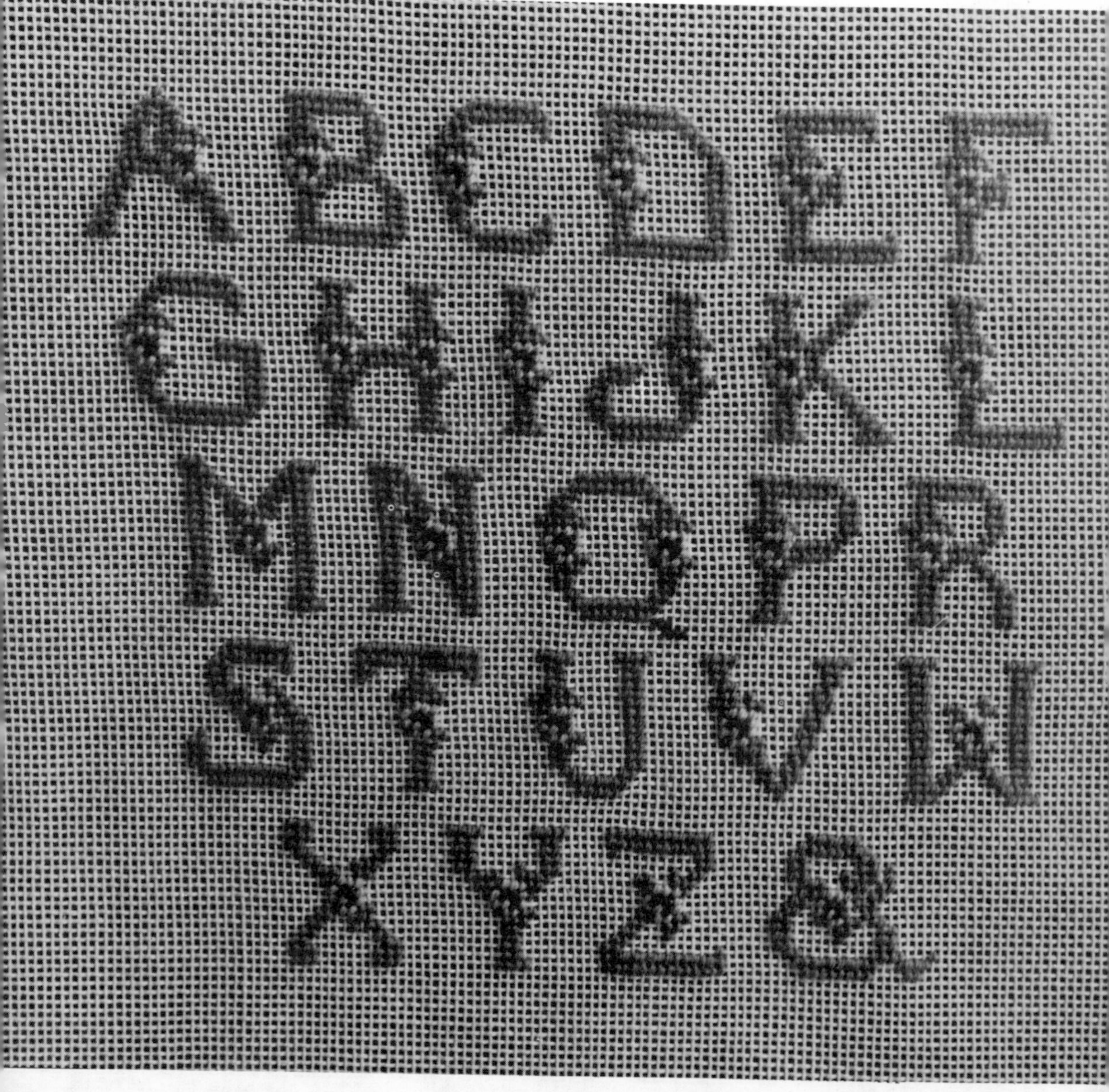

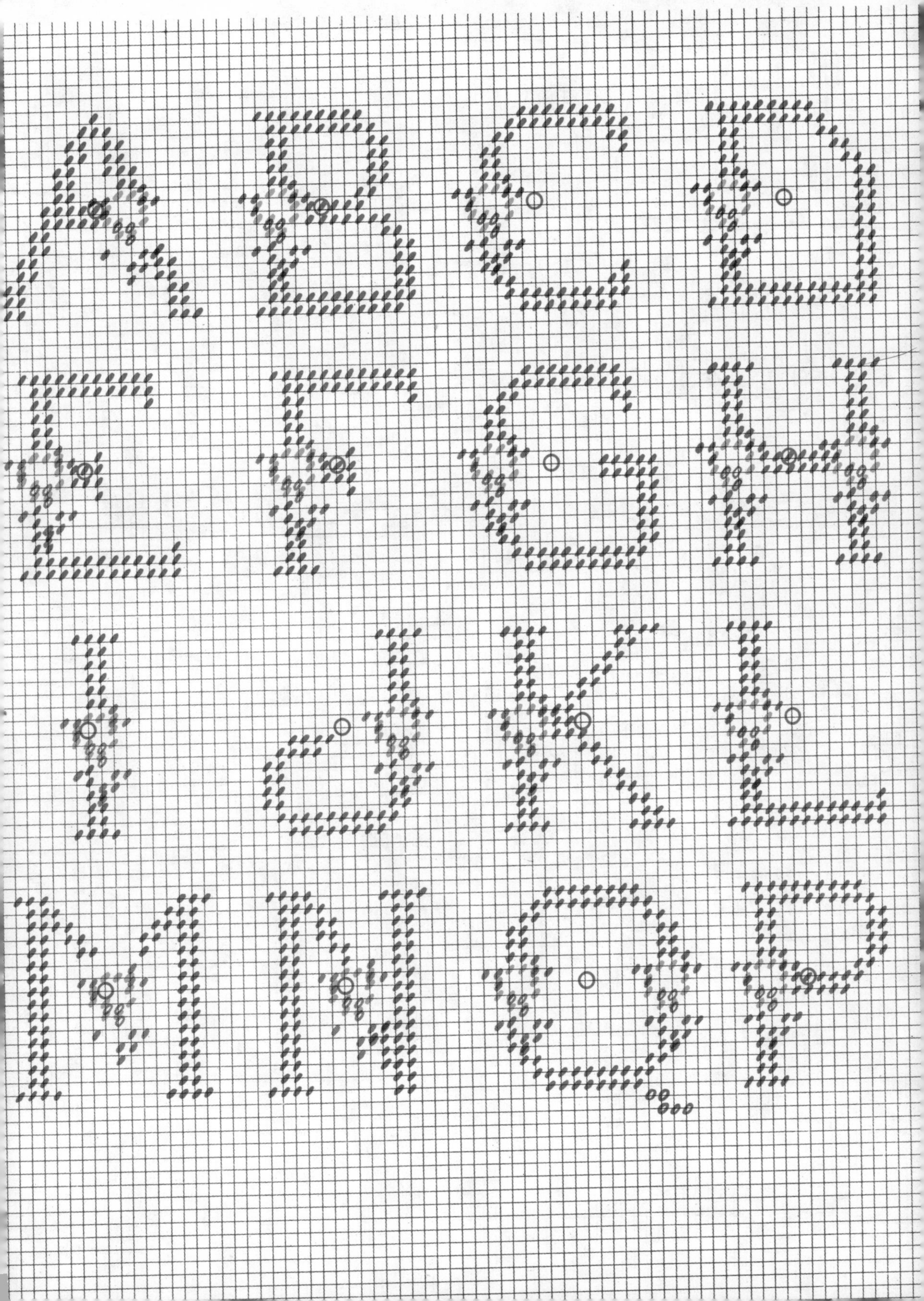

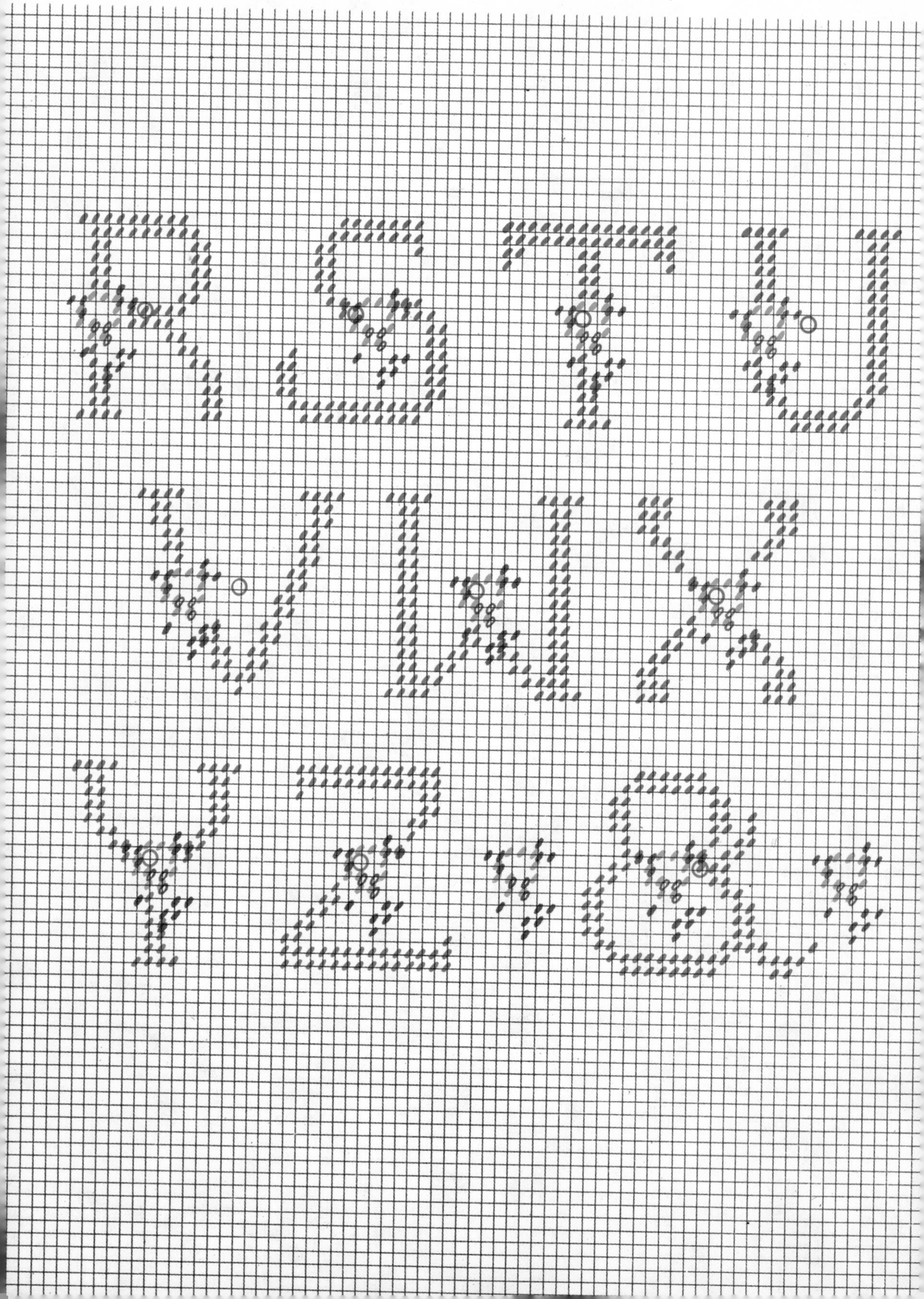

# CONTEMPORARY STRIPE

**Double strand on 14-ct. canvas**
**height: 16 threads**

This is a very bold, colorful alphabet that is excellent for monograms. Stitch the outline first and then fill in with the Stem stitch in a second color. A blow-up of a section of this letter design is shown here to help you get started. Make sure that the Stem stitches share holes with the Tent stitches, or canvas will show through. For an extra touch of decoration, a Backstitch in the outline color or a third color can be worked down the center of the Stem.

Contemporary Stripe letters appear in a color picture on page v.

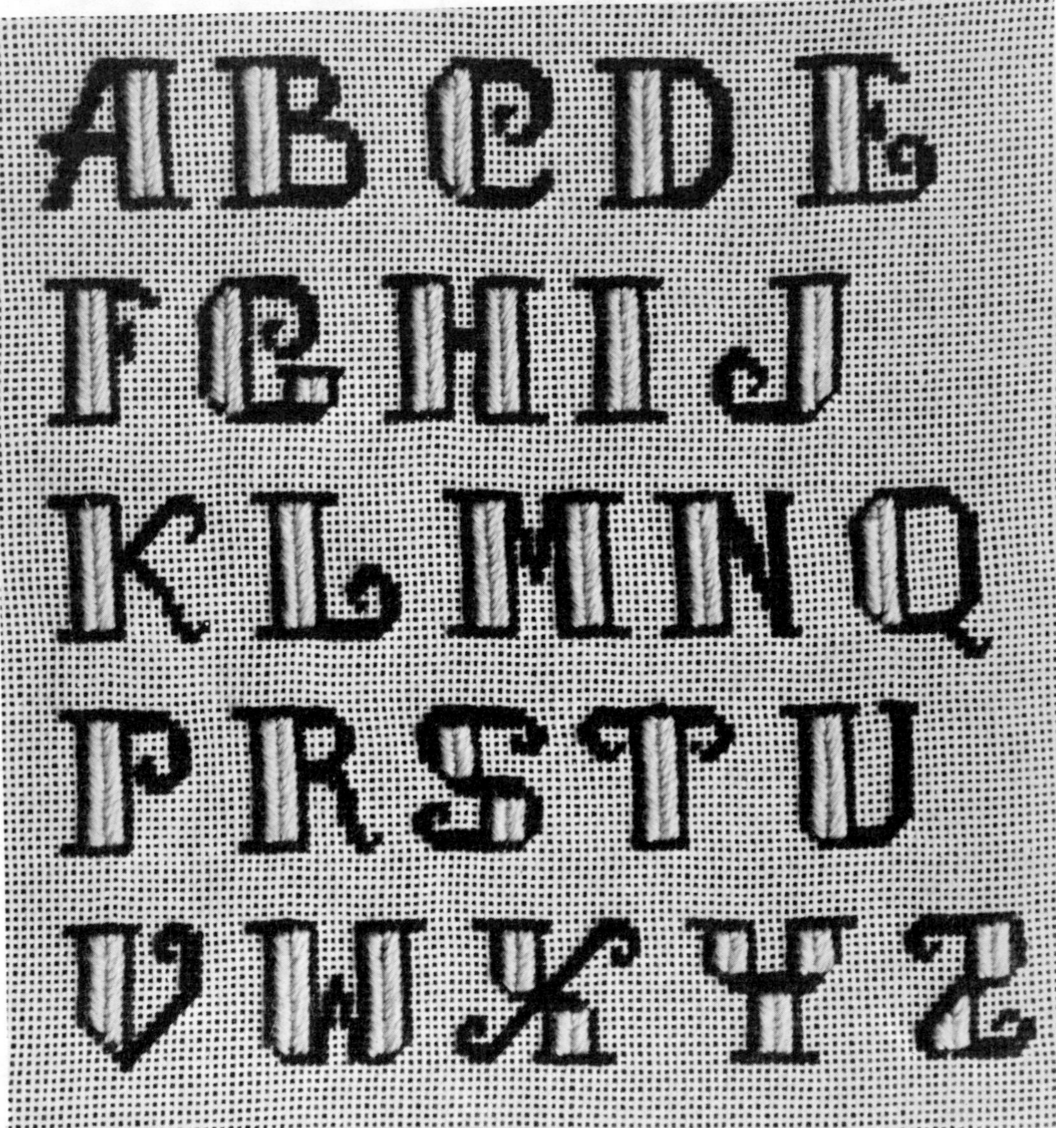

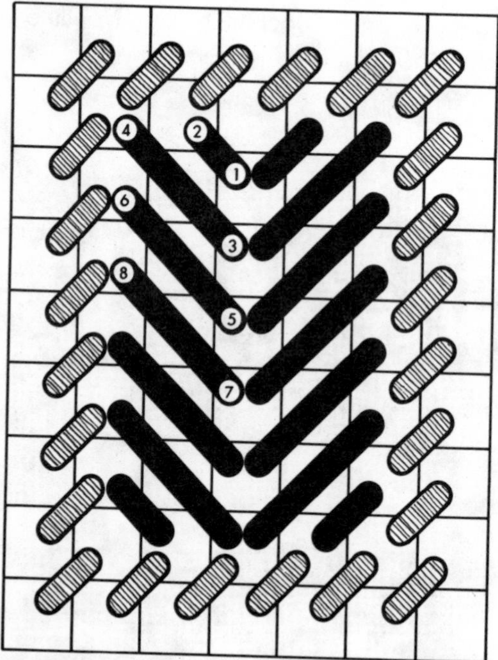


This diagram shows how the Contemporary Stripe letters are stitched. Stitch the Tent outline of the letter first and then fill in with Stem stitch, shown in black. The needle comes from back of canvas to front at 1 and to the back, ending the stitch, at 2.

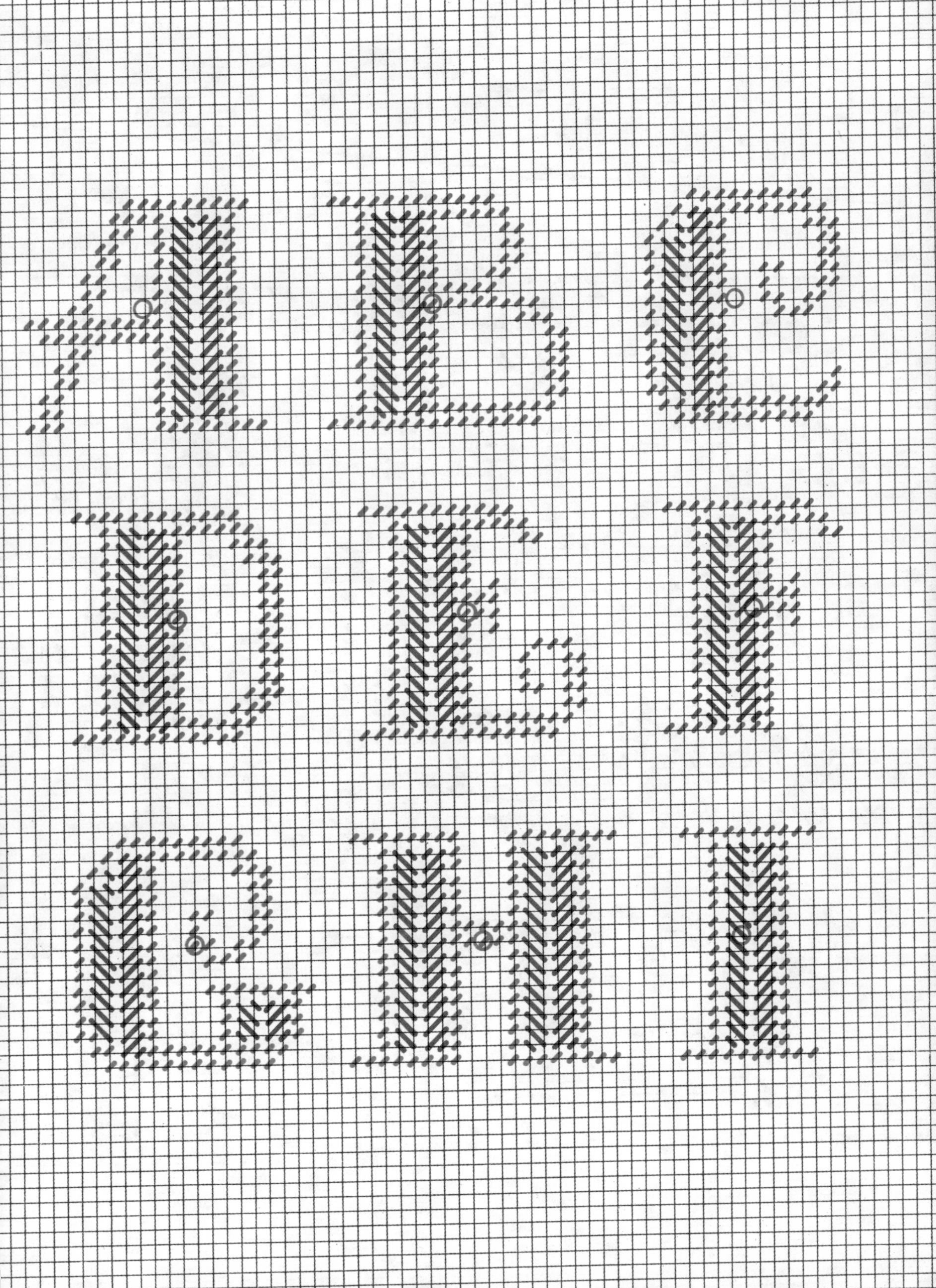

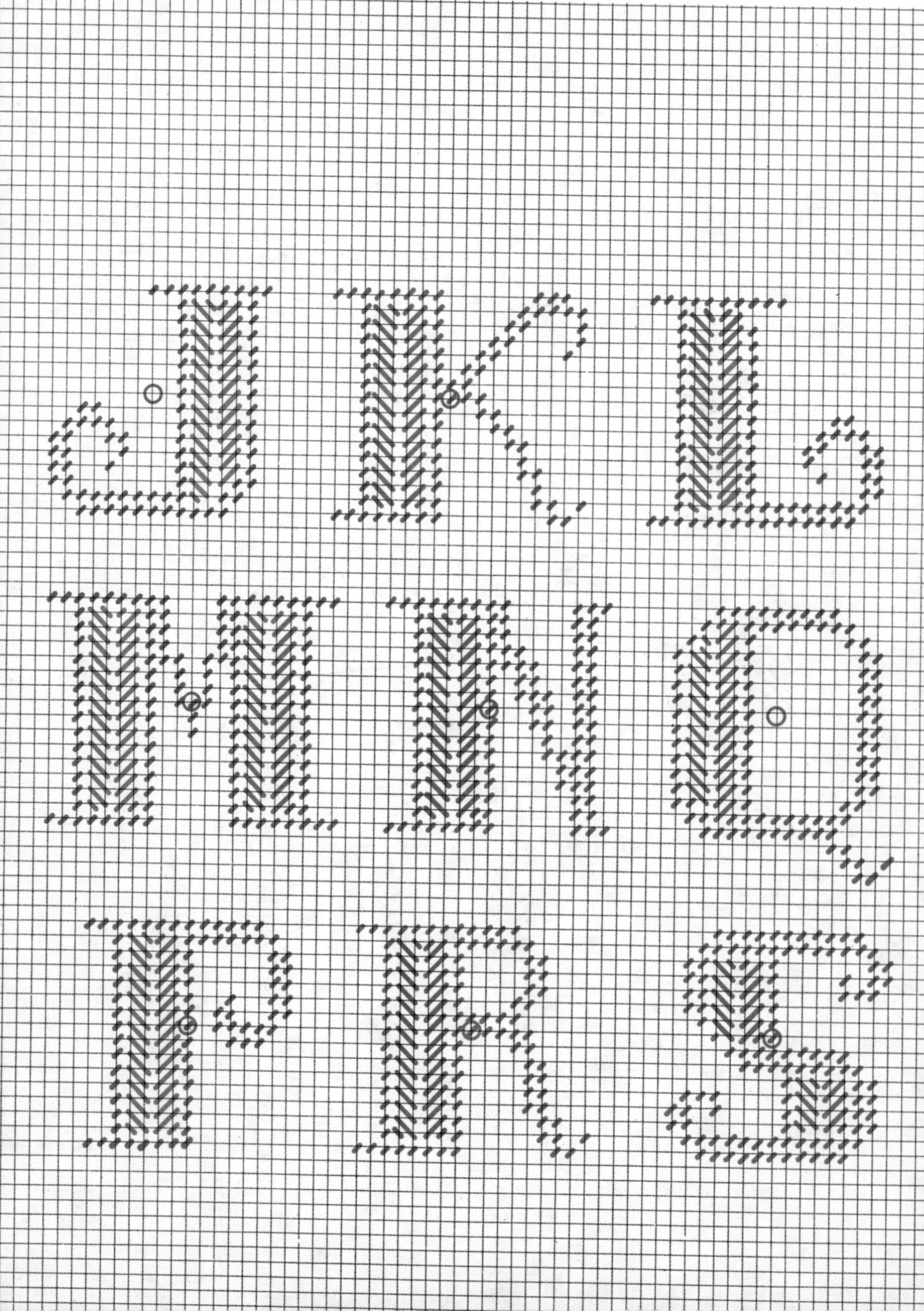

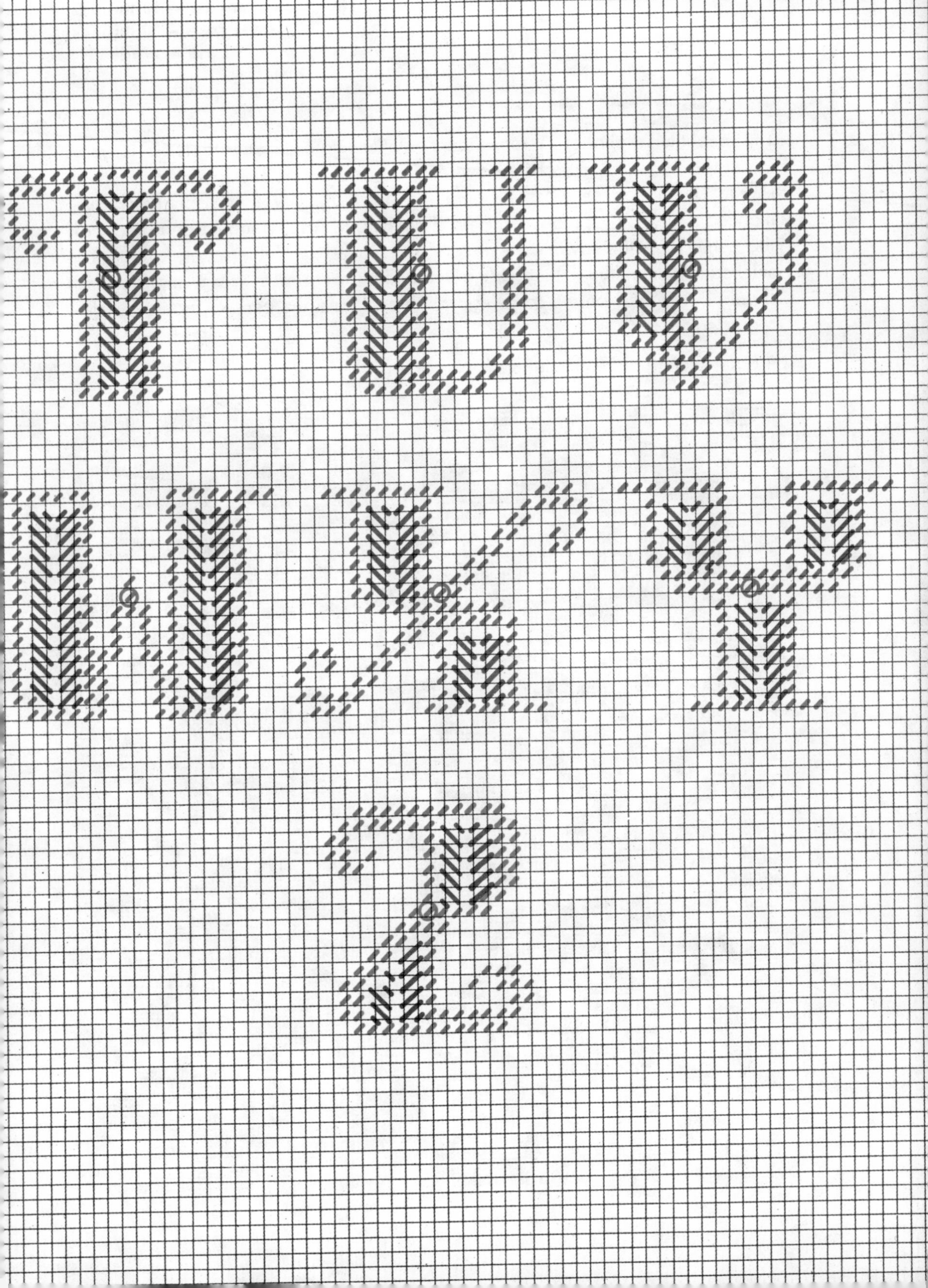

# GOTHIC

**Double strand on 14-ct. canvas**
**height: upper case – 18 threads**
**lower case – 10 threads**
**base average**

This beautiful alphabet is reminiscent of illuminated manuscripts. It is very useful for names, quotations, and in ecclesiastical work. The lower-case letters should be placed as close together as possible, and it is strongly recommended that you graph a word before stitching it. Also, it should be noted that the centers on the lower-case letters are placed as if the letters are to be stitched individually. If they are put together to form a word, the bottoms should be aligned on the same canvas thread, and the centers should be disregarded.

A color picture of Gothic letters is on page v.

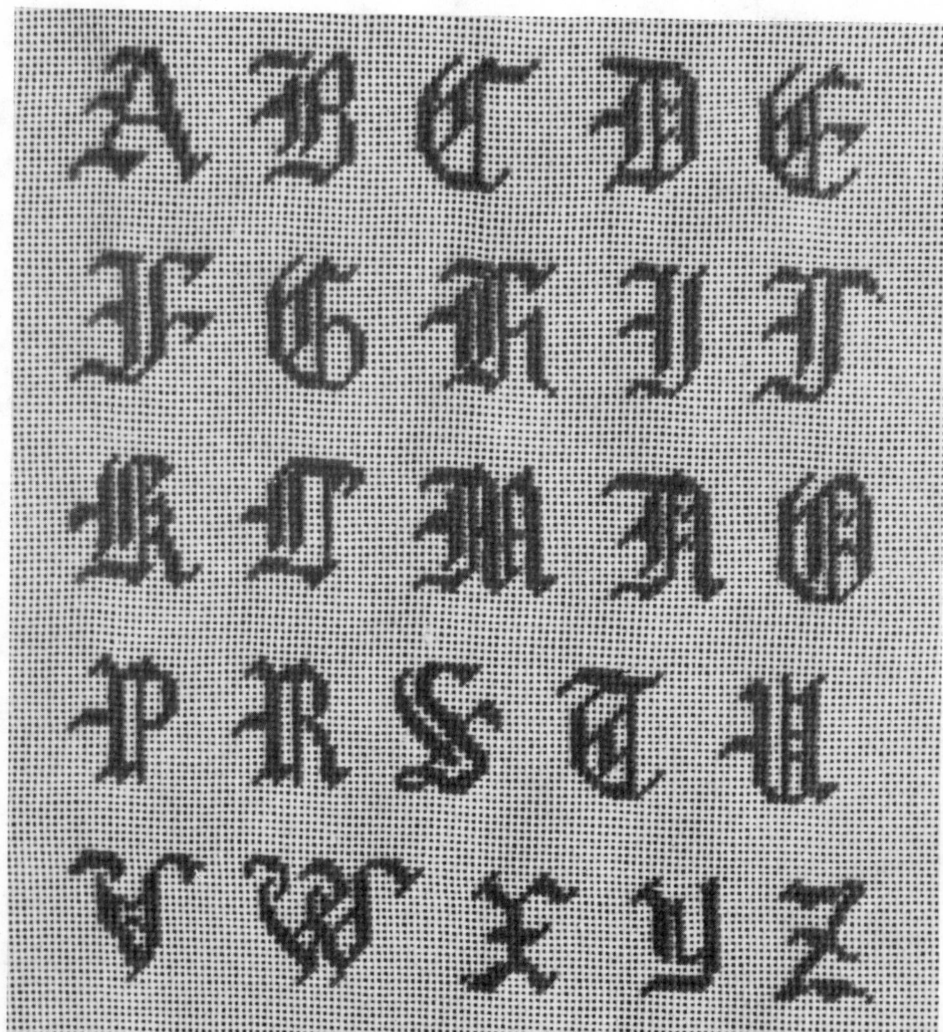

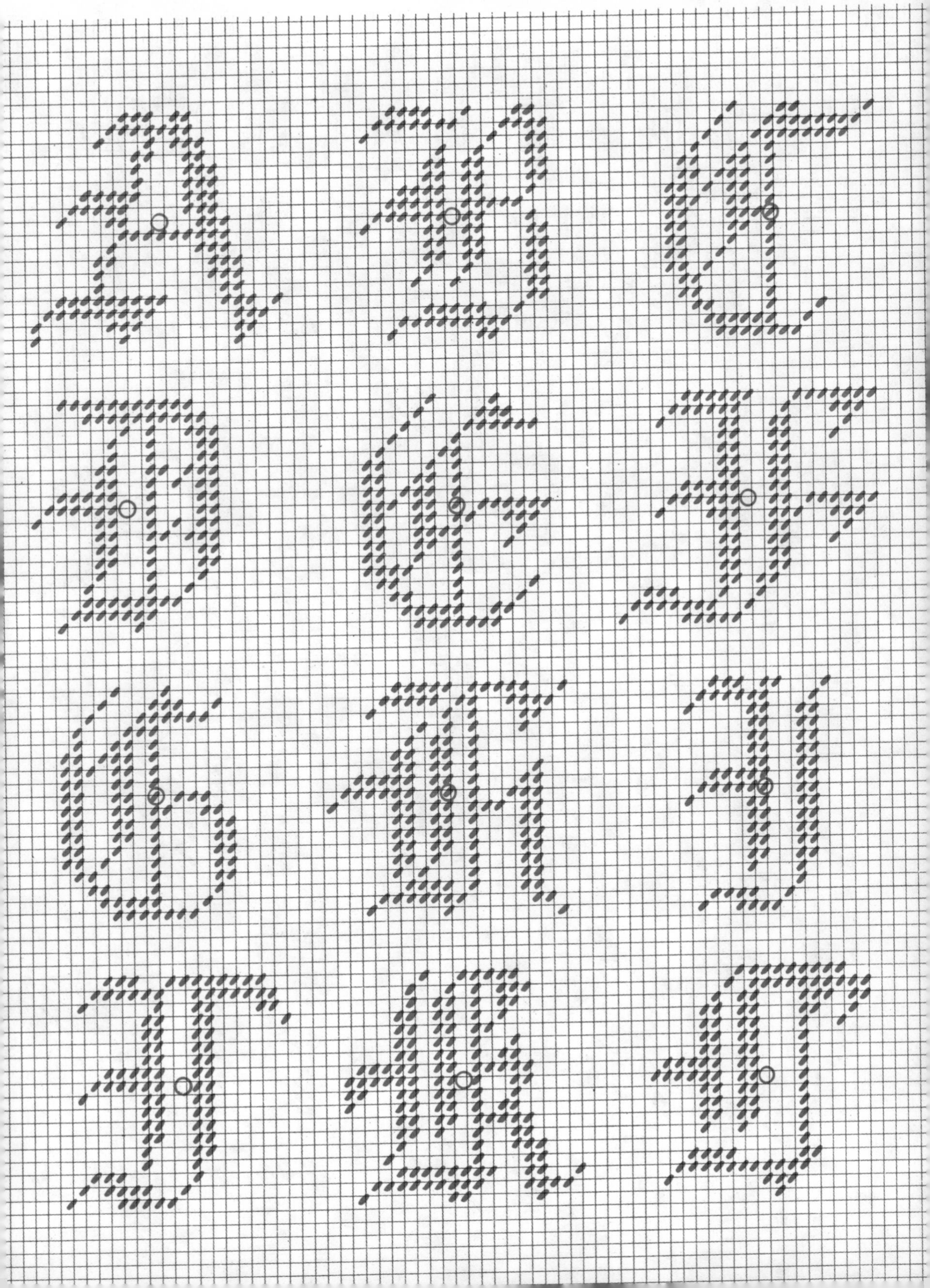

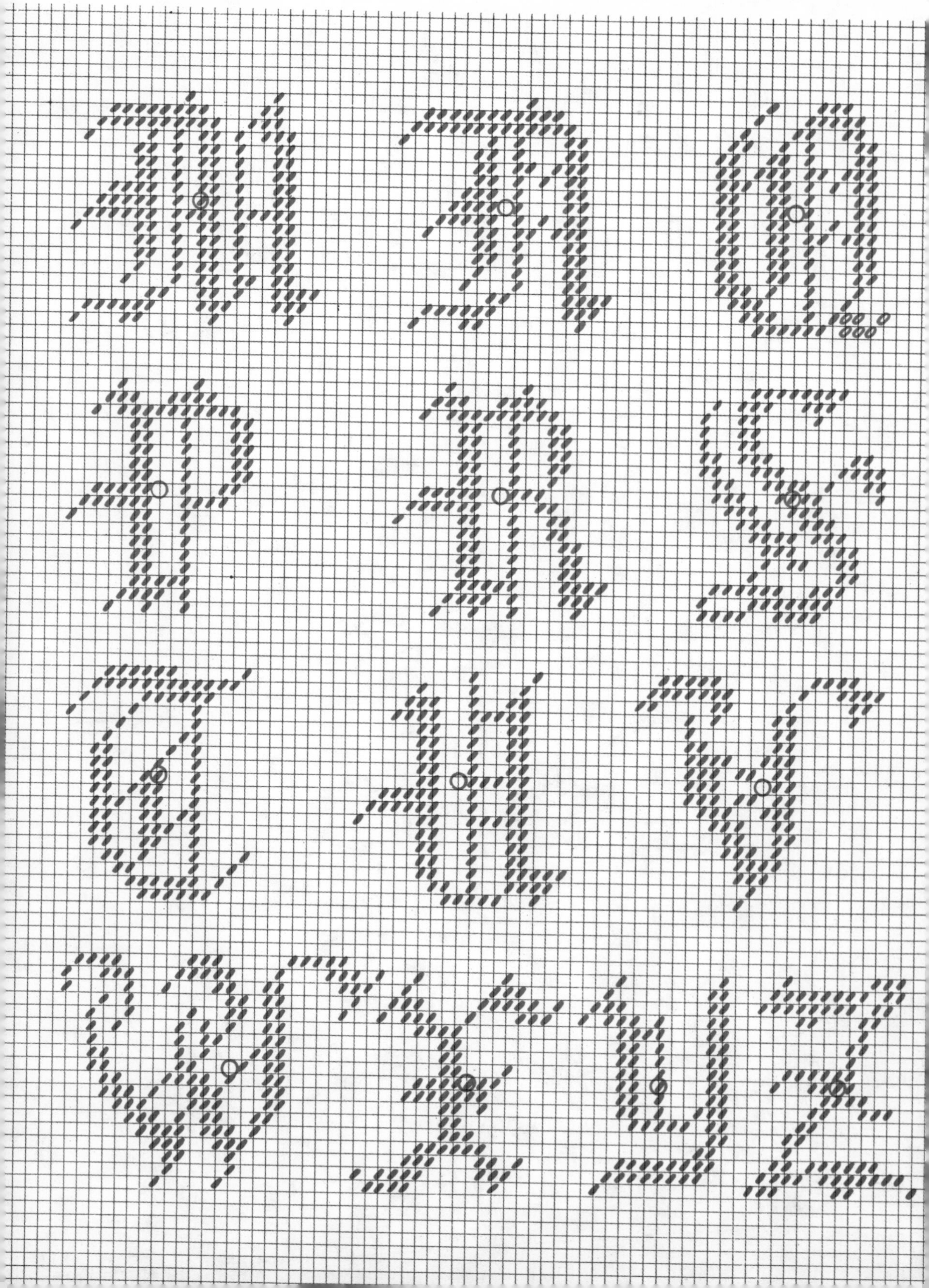

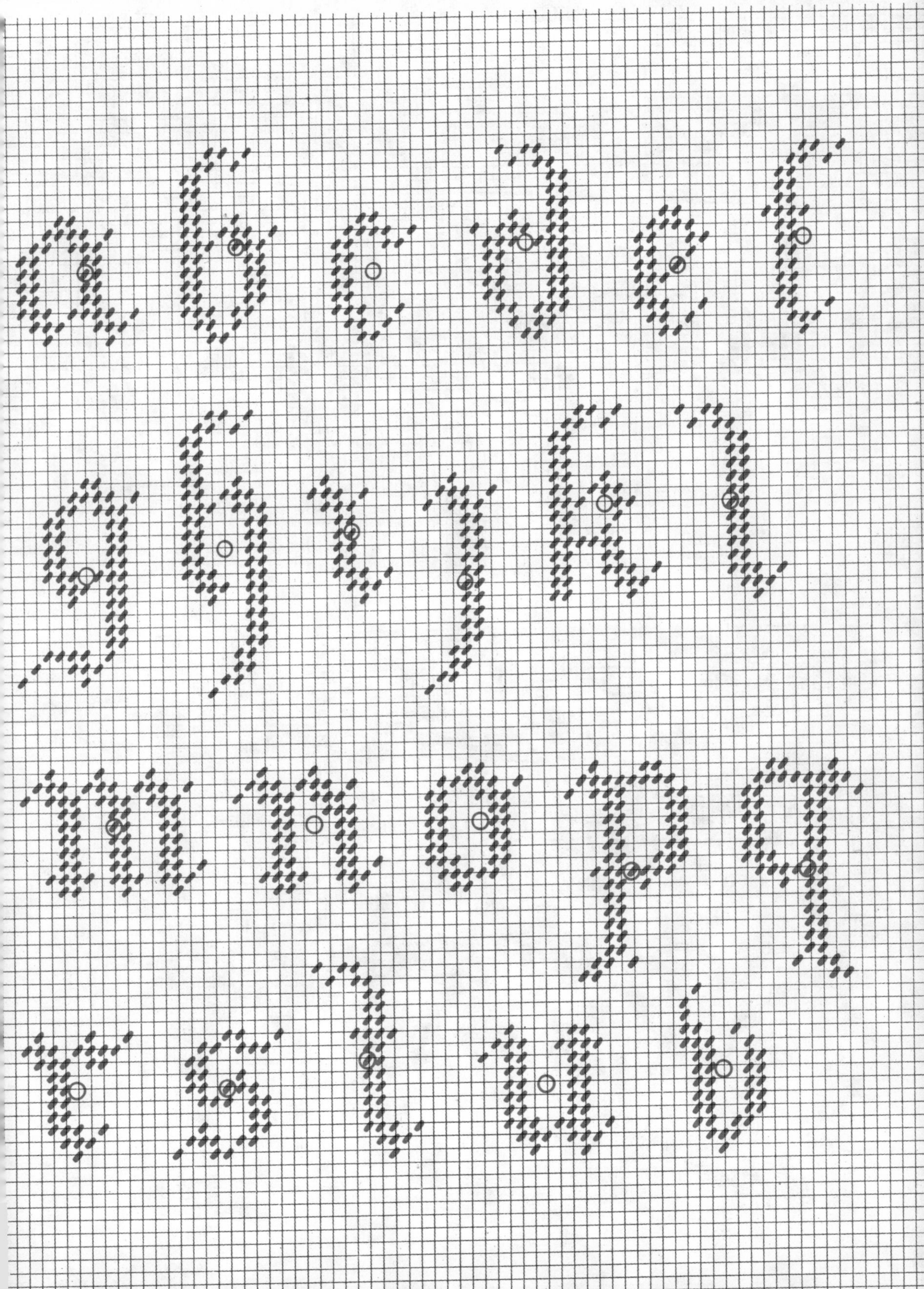

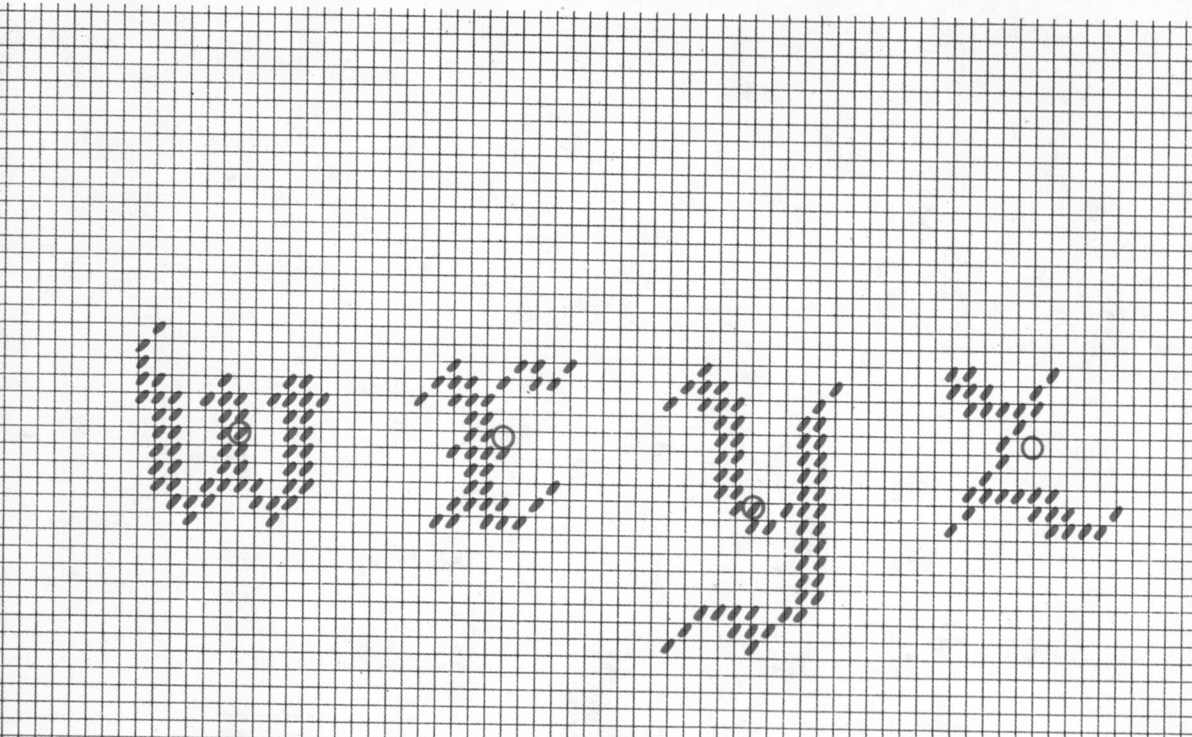

This tiny Wild Flower napkin ring makes an alluring gift. The Petit Point stitched piece is stuffed with a cotton ball and glued to a cardboard insert that fits the metal mounting.

A bold Bargello border surrounds an initial "S" designed by the stitcher. The letter is embellished with a scrolling vine worked in Chain stitch.

This lucite ice bucket was designed as a wedding gift. The Roman Magesty "T" features the Garden of Eden serpent with rhinestone eye. International Alphabet Flags represent the couple's initials, their first names are worked in Lilliputian, the year of the marriage is in Roman Numerals, and a border message is worked in International Morse Code. Vine motifs from the Roman Magesty "T" are repeated as further decoration and to tie the design together. The piece is backed with green-and-white pillow ticking, and a lucite liner separates the needlepoint from the ice.

The framing of this cocktail recipe adds an elegant touch to the attractively designed piece. Several stitches have been incorporated for texture. Note the letters worked in Chain stitch off the grid of the canvas.

The green sailcloth purse uses a lower case script "a" in three positions to create an abstract design. Texture is introduced by using a different stitch in each background "compartment." The totebag sports an interlaced ribbon pattern using many canvas embroidery stitches. The initials are worked in an ornate script style.

A collage of letters forms the design for this purse panel in process. The areas have been marked off, and a variety of bright colors is used to stitch the cheery alphabet sampler.

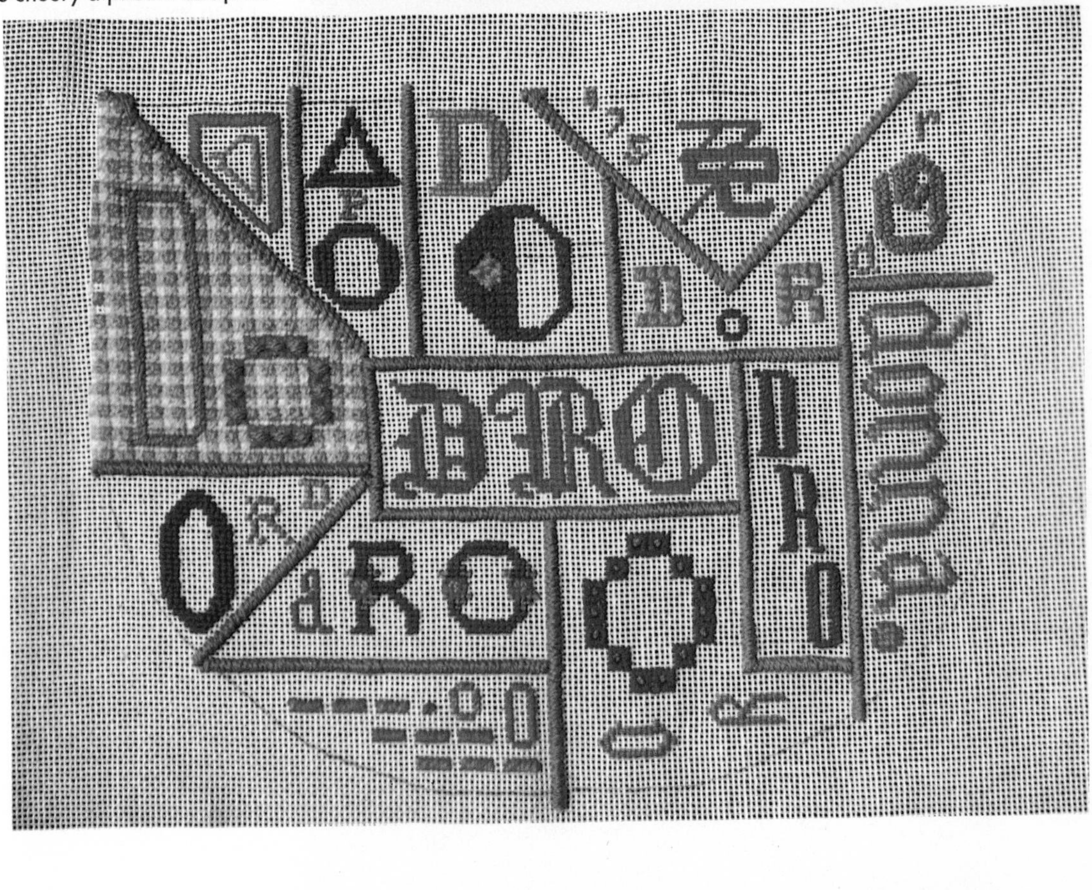

The pillow at the left incorporates many stitches to make needlepoint ribbons in soft pastels that interlace and turn gracefully at the edges. As much careful counting goes into laying out the ribbon pattern as goes into working letters and numbers. The Roman Magesty "B" has been worked in a variety of stitches and then mounted as a pillow insert in moire.

This pillow, mounted in pink velvet, has a Roman Magesty "D" insert stitched in Tent. The design is simple and straightforward, although highly textured and decorative.

# VICTORIAN EYELET

**Single strand on 14-ct. canvas**
**height: letters and numbers – 28 threads**

This alphabet is based on the large letters found on Victorian samplers and is a "giant" version of the Early Sampler letters on page 60. The letters are composed of Eyelet (Algerian Eye) stitches in an ornate style. The bizarre "A" is often seen on heritage samplers as an alternate for the more readable one, shown in the stitched alphabet. While the alphabet is somewhat limited because of its large size, it can be quite effective in projects where a single letter is required.

A diagram of the Eyelet stitch is shown on the next page. It is very important that you start each stitch at the outside of the unit and work down into the center (C on the diagram) to keep from snagging your work. Remember to use a single strand on 14-ct. canvas.

Other stitch units that will fit the 4 by 4 thread spaces are Crossed Corners and Smyrna (page 93).

A color picture using Victorian Eyelet is found on page iii.

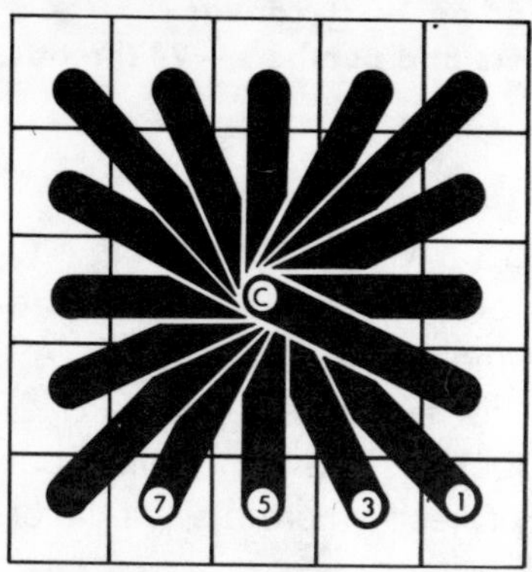


Each Eyelet unit covers a 4-thread square. It is convenient to start in the lower right corner, bringing the yarn to the surface of the canvas at 1 and going to the back at "C" (center). All your stitches should be worked from the outside of the unit down into the middle to prevent snagging. Remember to use a single strand of yarn on 14-ct. canvas or the stitches will become very bulky. The diagrams of the letters are shown blocked off on the following pages.

Parallel rows of Eyelet units are used to make a double "O" as the design for this ornate mini-picture. The Eyelet stitches have been outlined with metallic thread, and three different stitches add texture to the background.

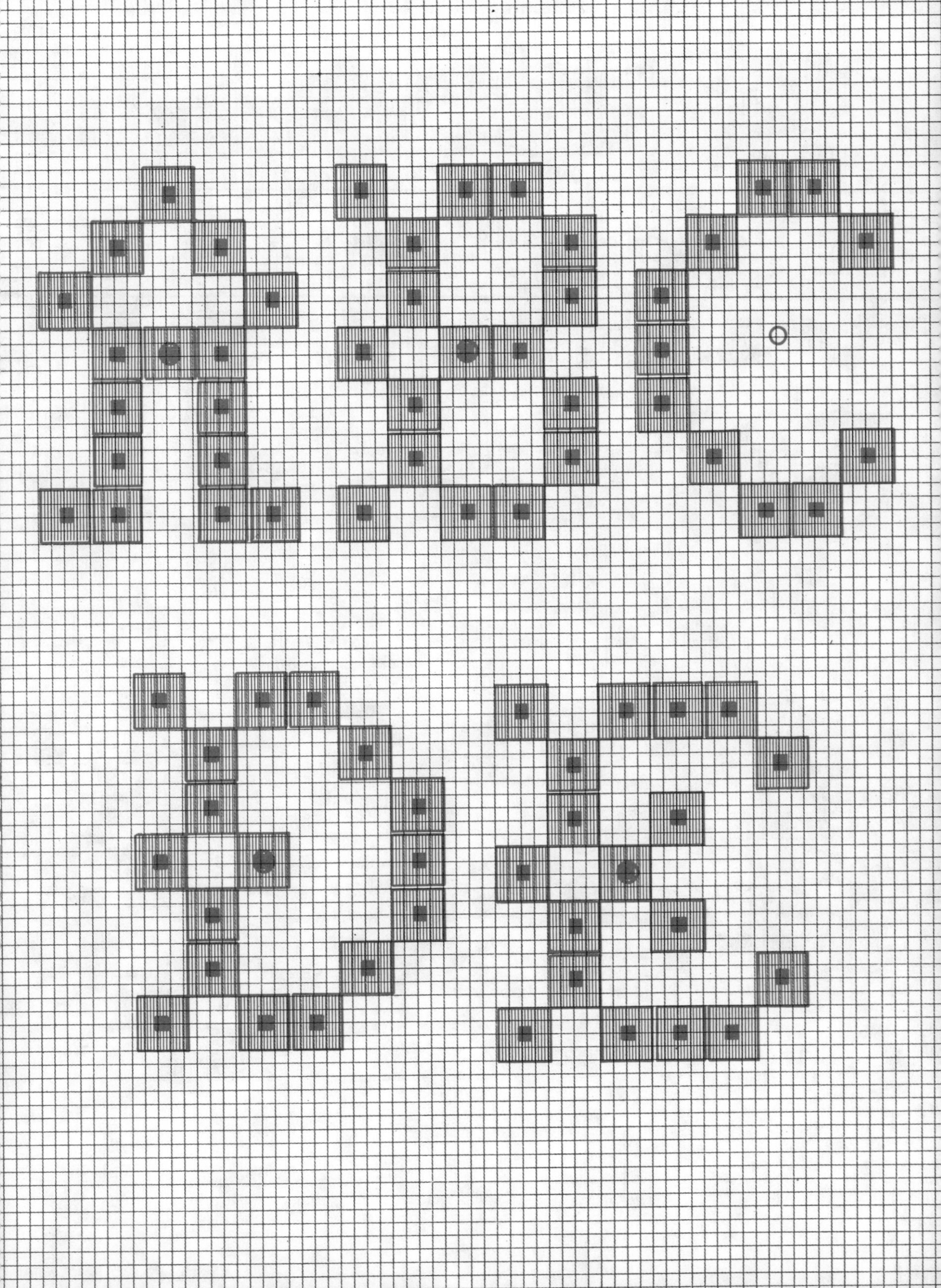

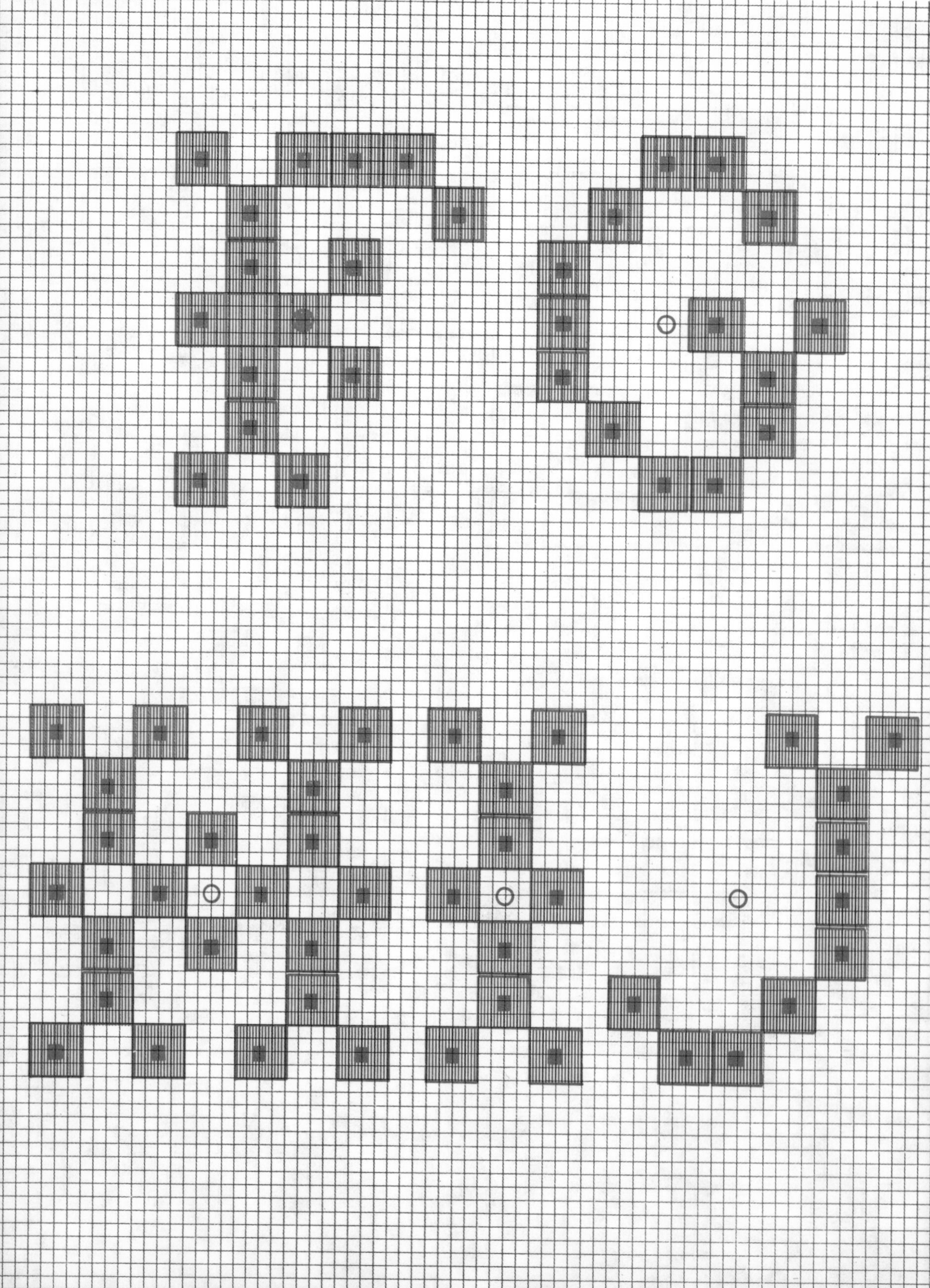

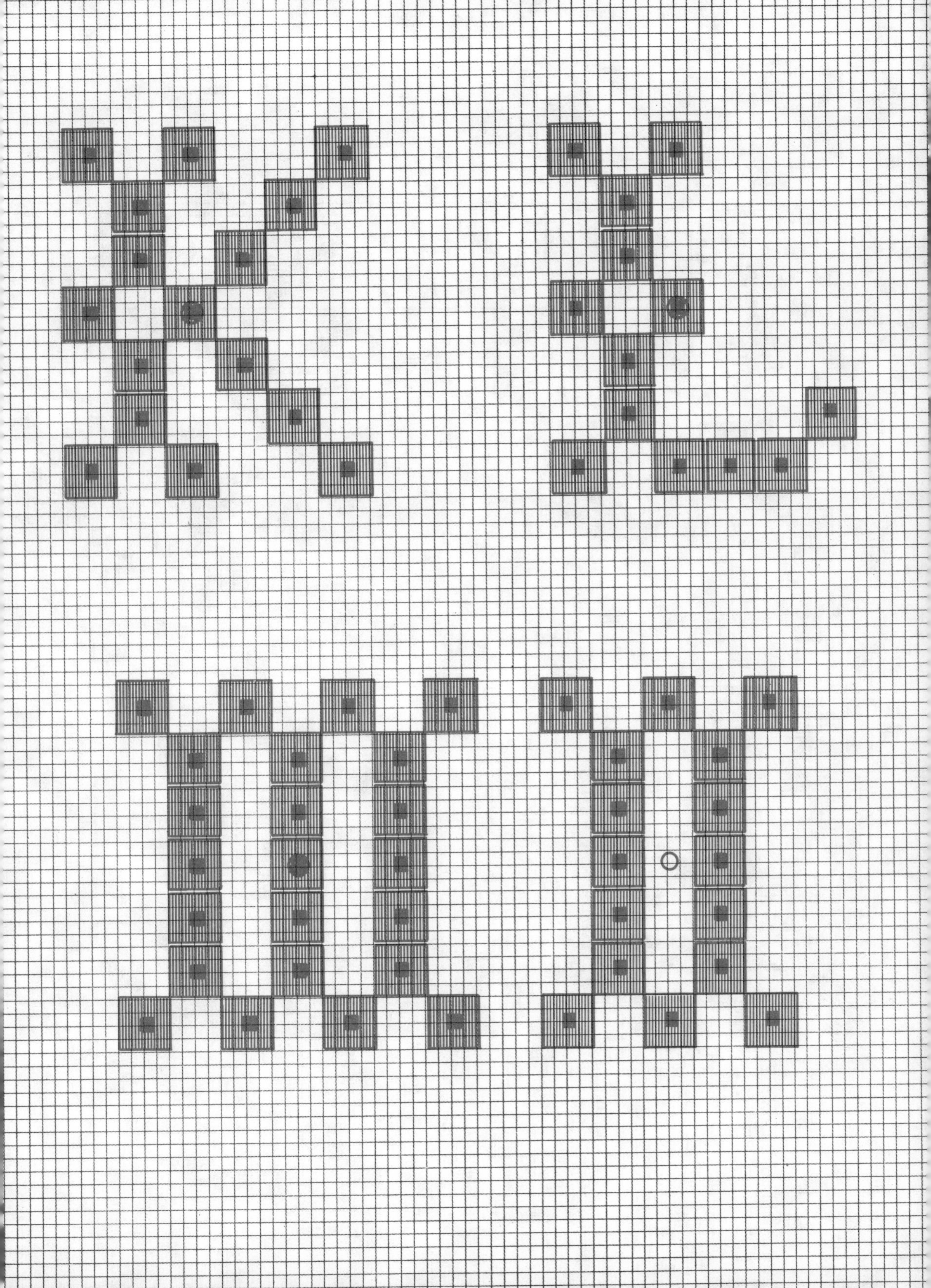

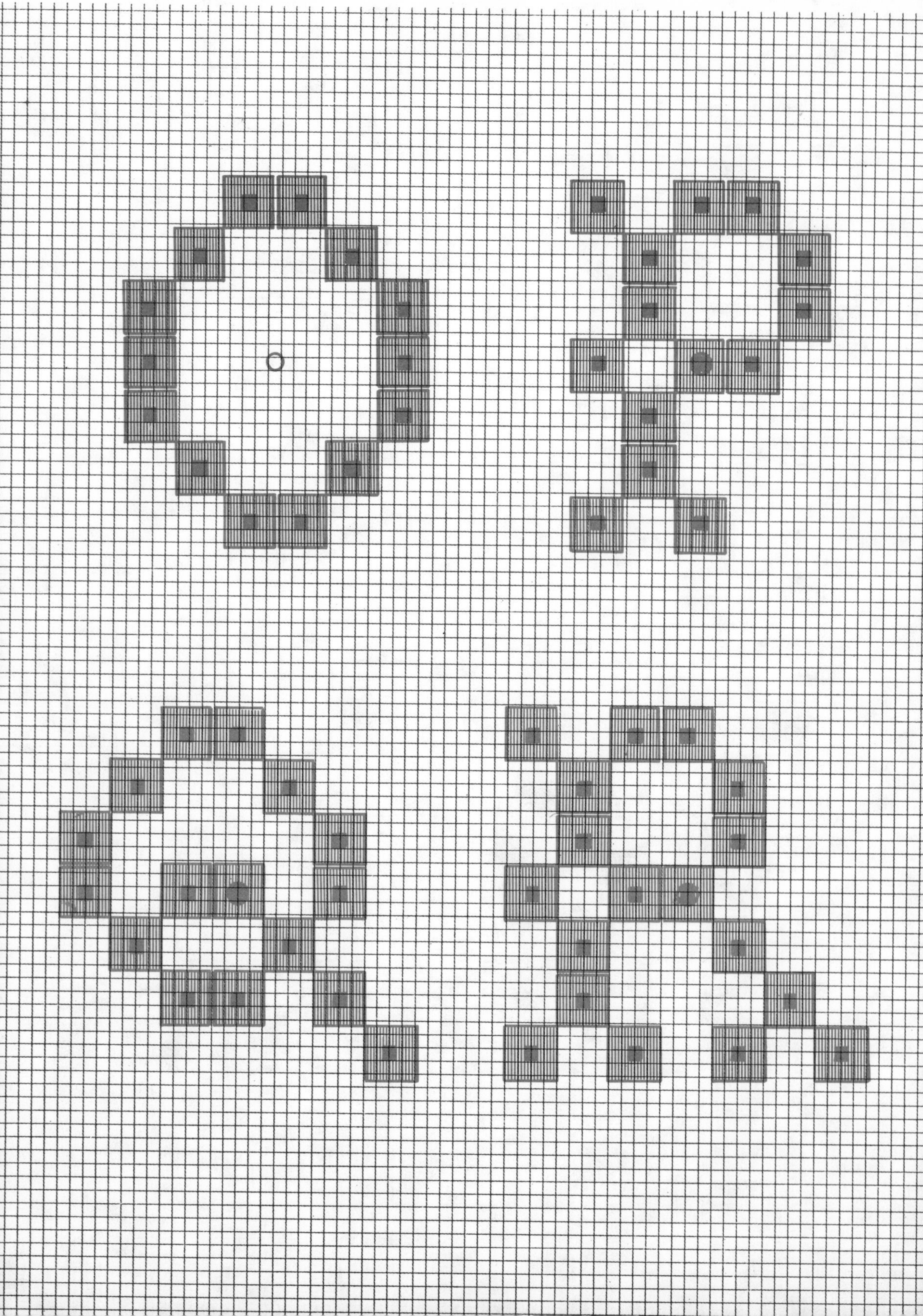

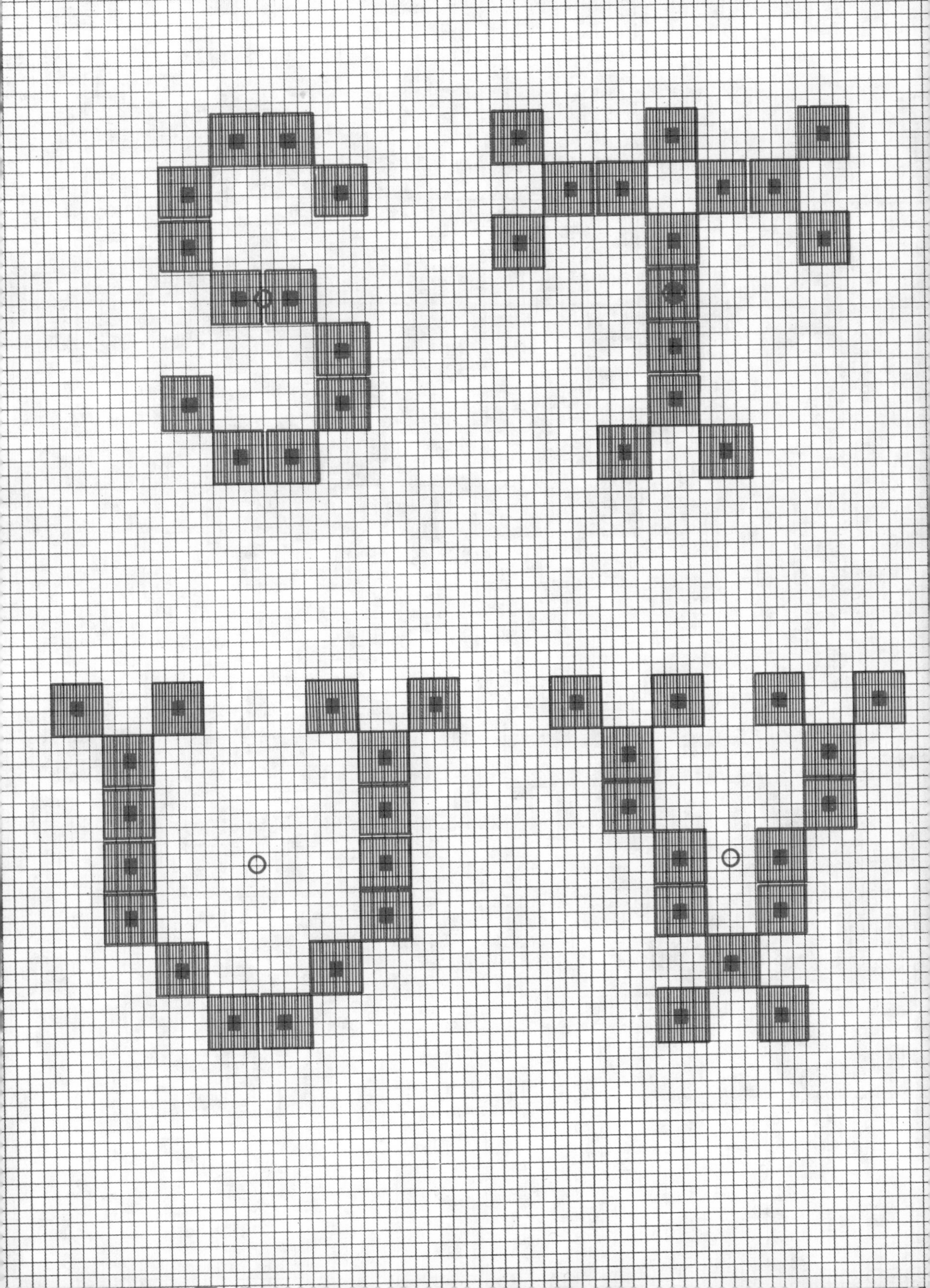

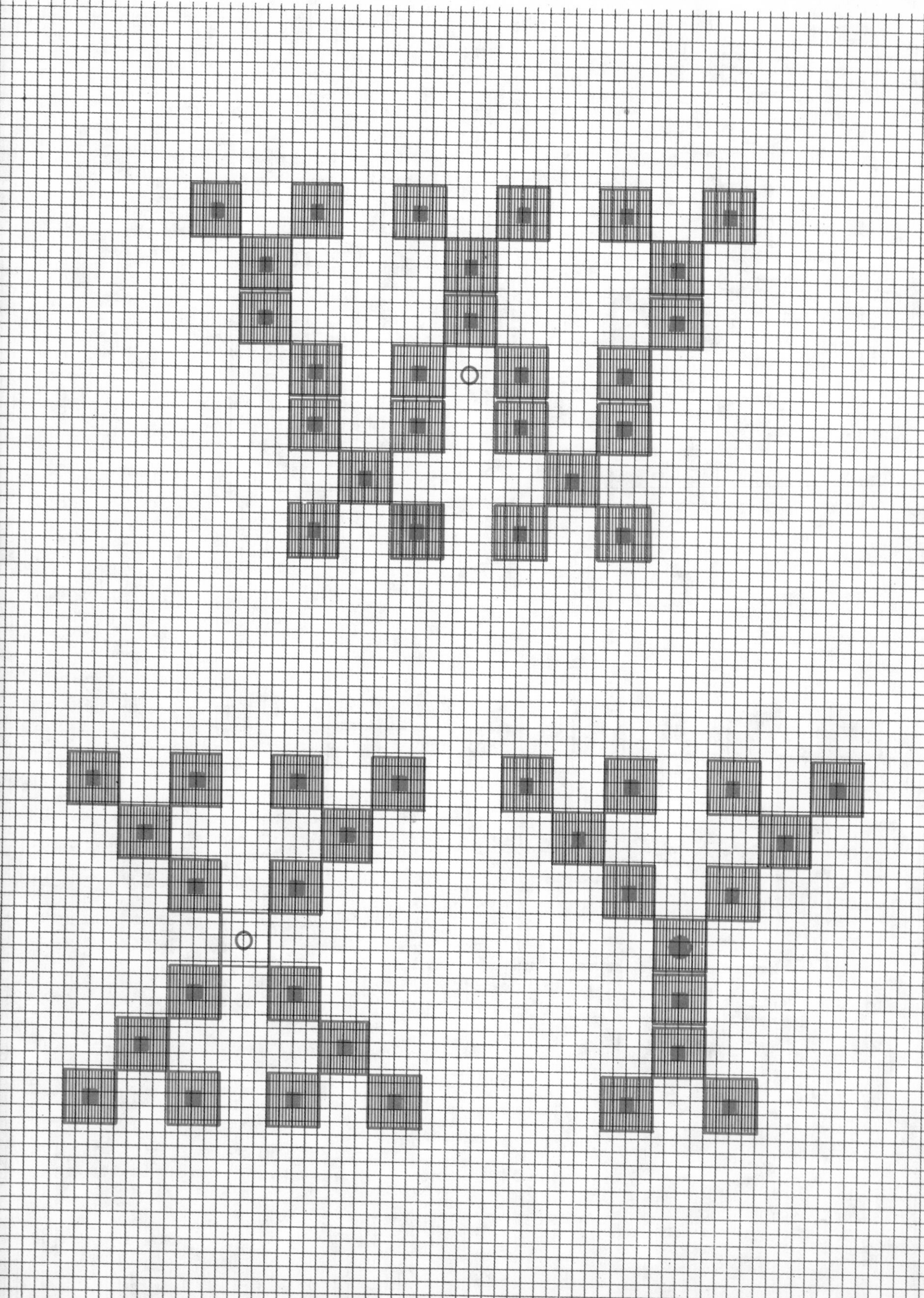

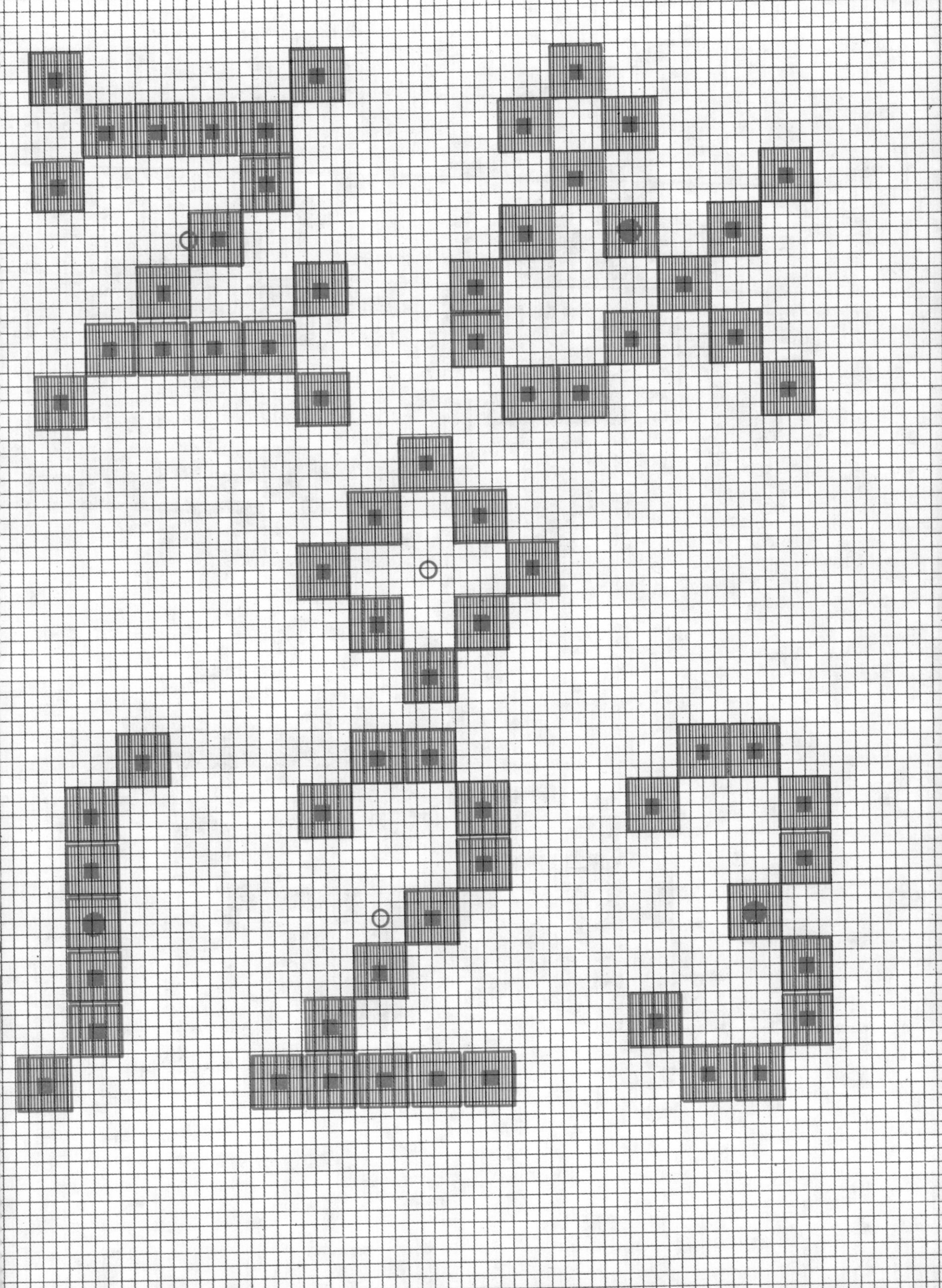

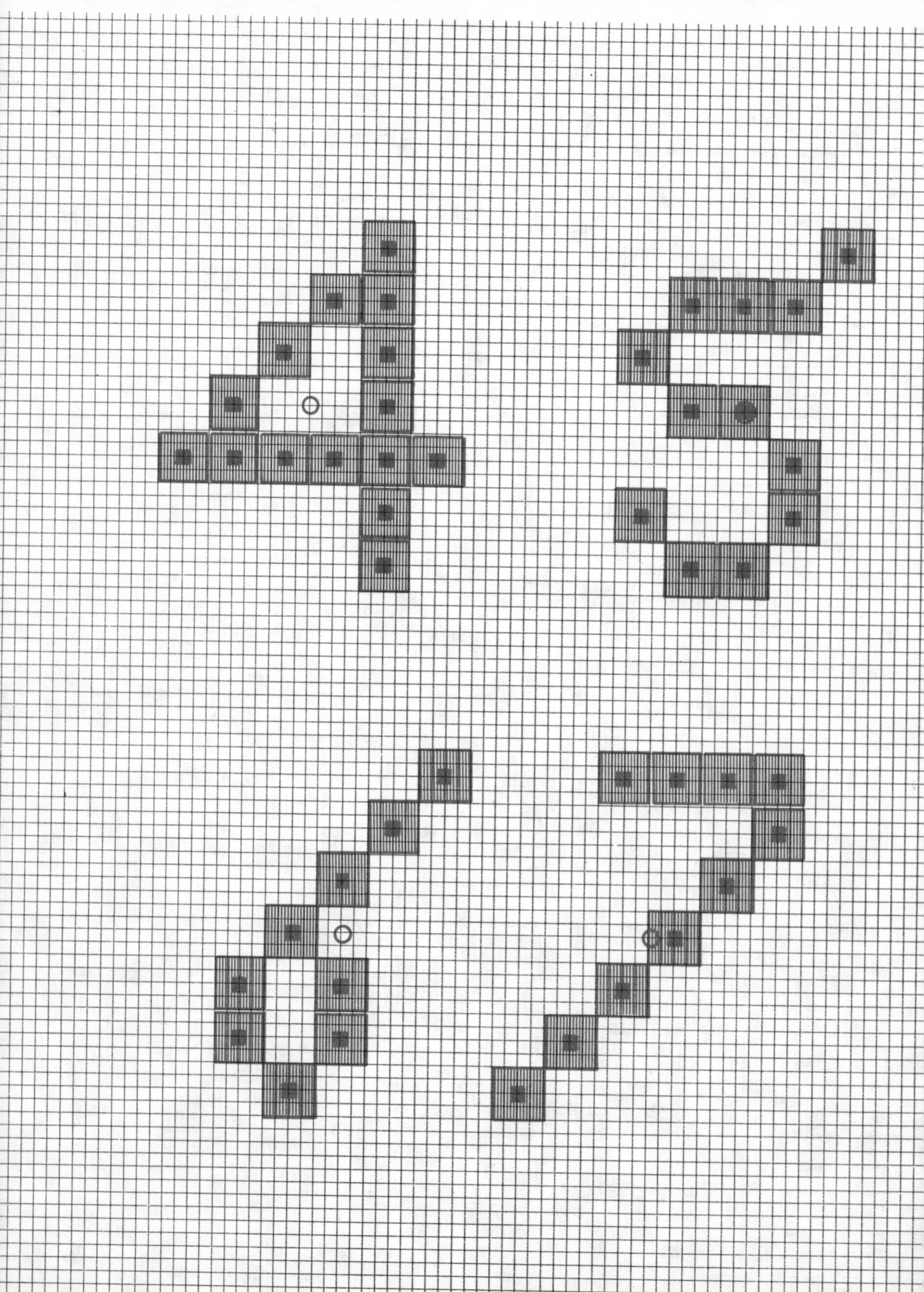

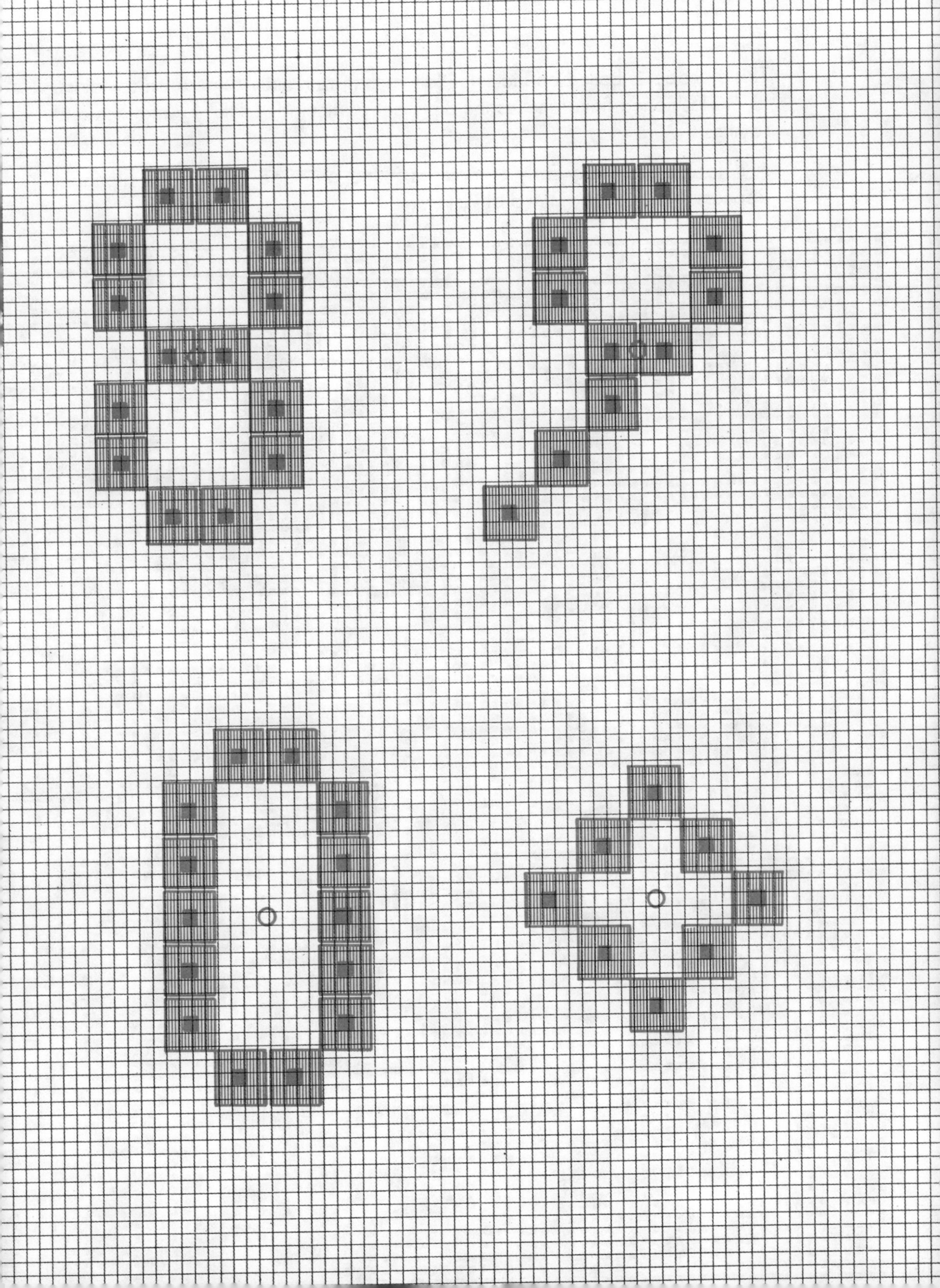

# EARLY SAMPLER

**Double strand on 14-ct. canvas**
**height: 8 threads**

This alphabet is based on the small letters that frequently appear on samplers. Its old-fashioned flavor makes the alphabet particularly useful for mottoes and sayings.

A color picture using Early Sampler is found on page viii and the alphabet appears on the back of the dust jacket.

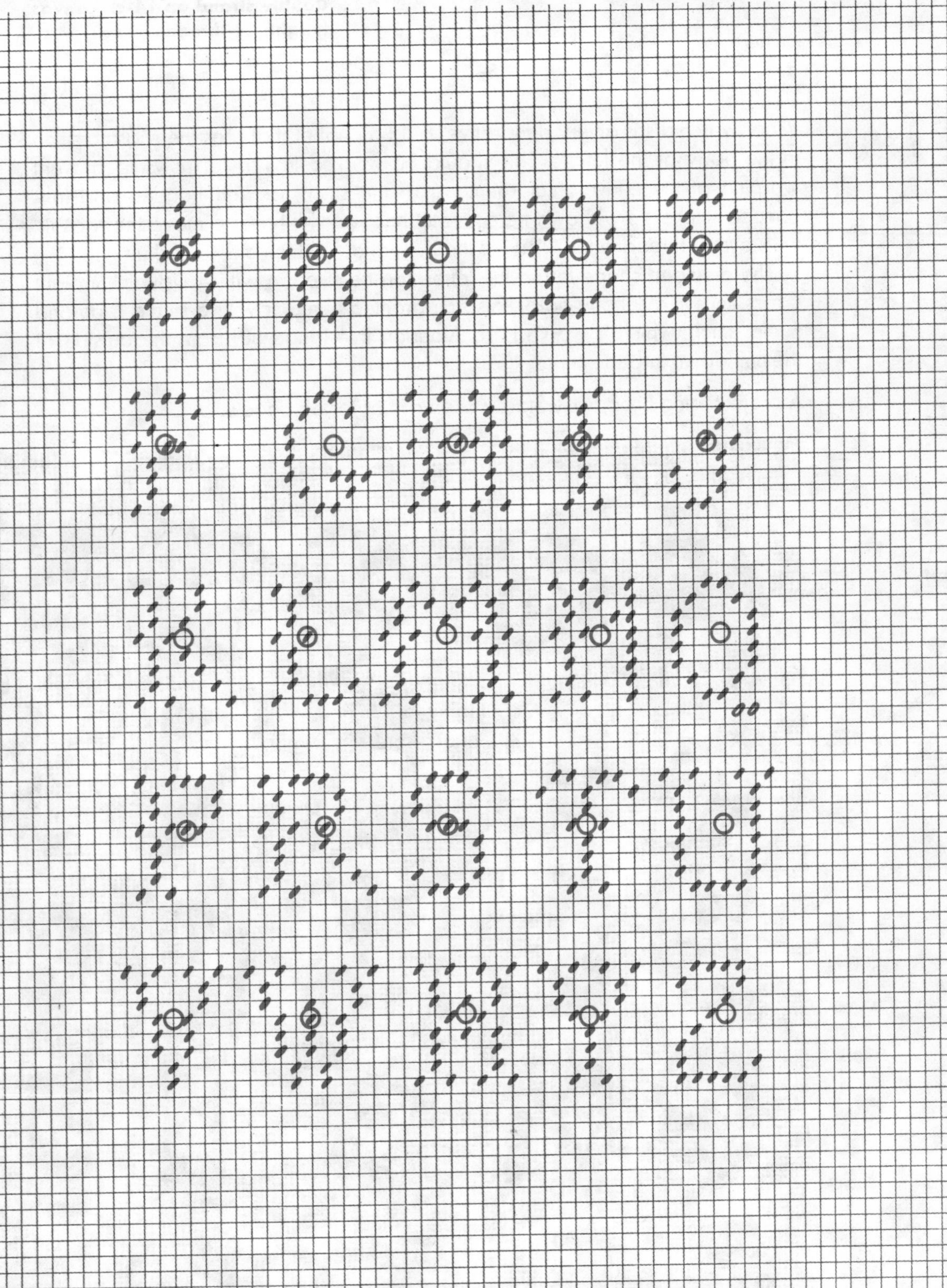

# BROADWAY STARS

**Double strand on 14-ct. canvas**
**height: 24 threads**

Broadway Stars is a very decorative, bold alphabet that uses the Mosaic stitch in the body of the letters. This should be worked in vertical rows to prevent warping of the canvas. Enlargements of the stitch for right-handed and left-handed stitchers are shown here. Note that you will have to move the Mosaic units over 1 thread when working the X, Y, and Z, which are on a slant.

The diamond shape left in the letter can be filled in with 4 Double Straight Cross units in a second color, also diagramed here, or with a single Diamond Eyelet stitch, which is worked like Algerian Eye (page 50) from the outside of the unit down into the center (C).

A project using Broadway Stars is shown in color on page v.

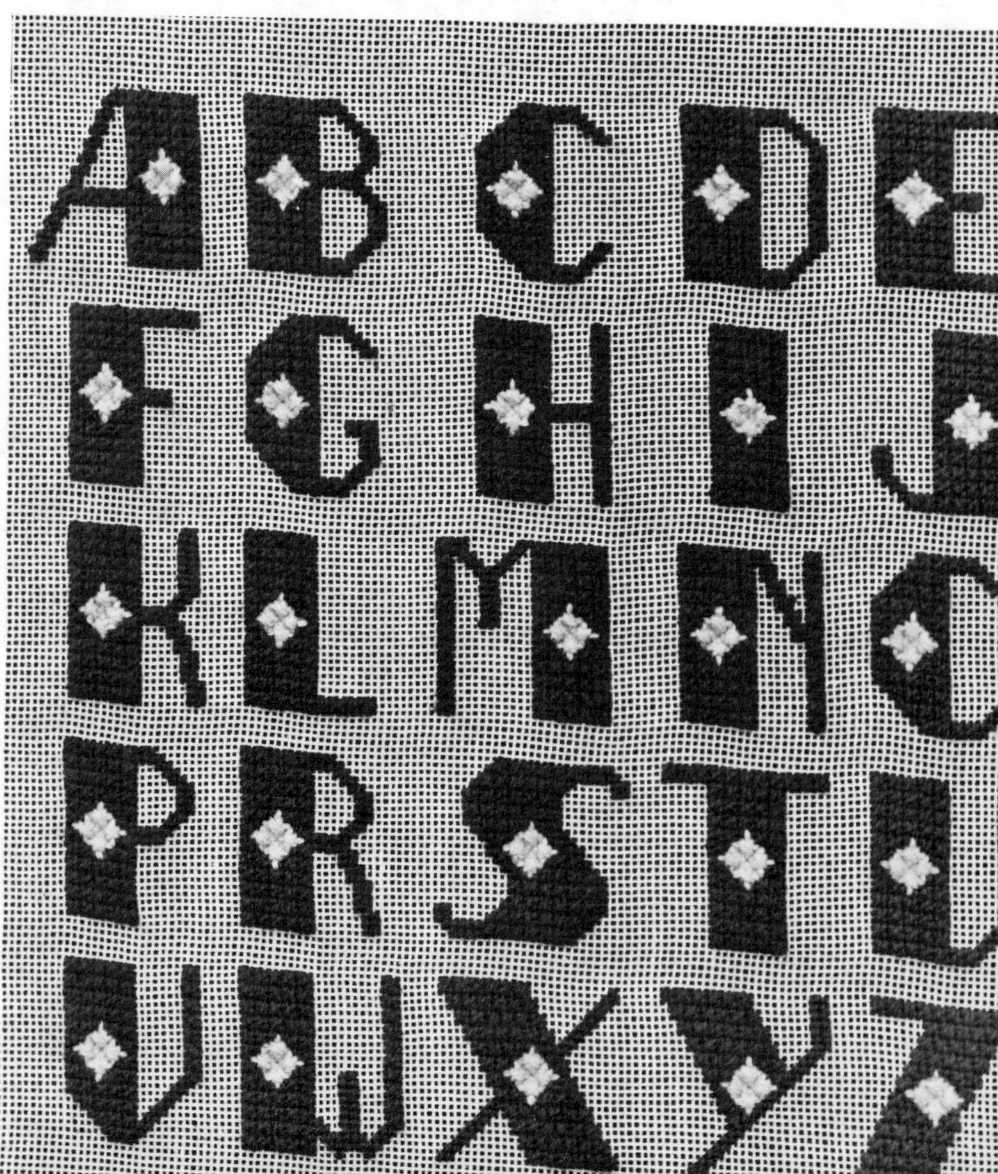

## MOSAIC

RIGHT-HANDED STITCHERS

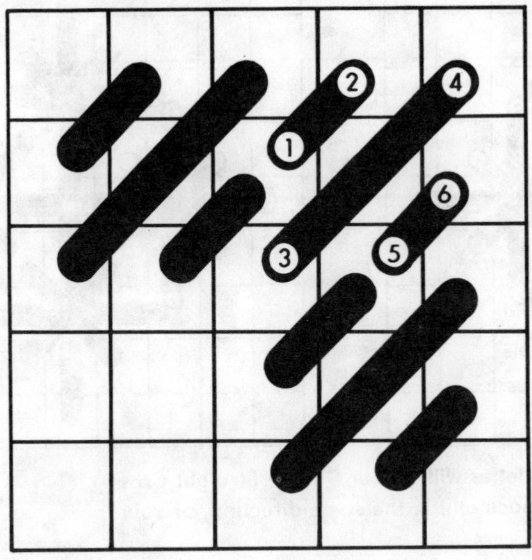


LEFT-HANDED STITCHERS

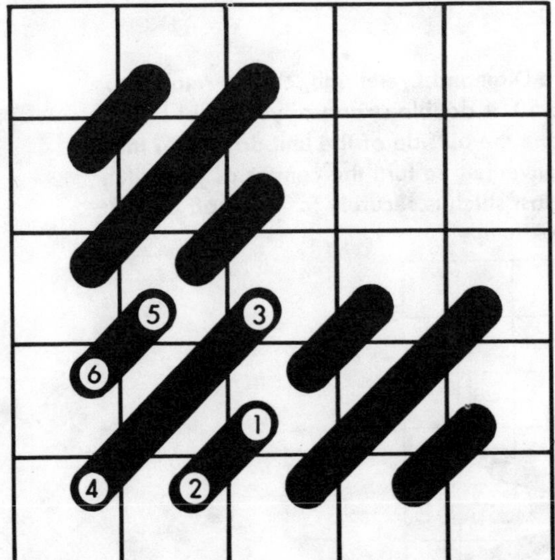


The body of the Broadway Star letter is made up of Mosaic stitches worked vertically to prevent warping. The diagrams here show the numbering for right-handed and left-handed stitchers. Stitches begin at odd numbers (come to the surface of the canvas with the yarn at 1, and so on) and end at even numbers (yarn goes to back of canvas).

## DOUBLE STRAIGHT CROSS

RIGHT-HANDED STITCHERS

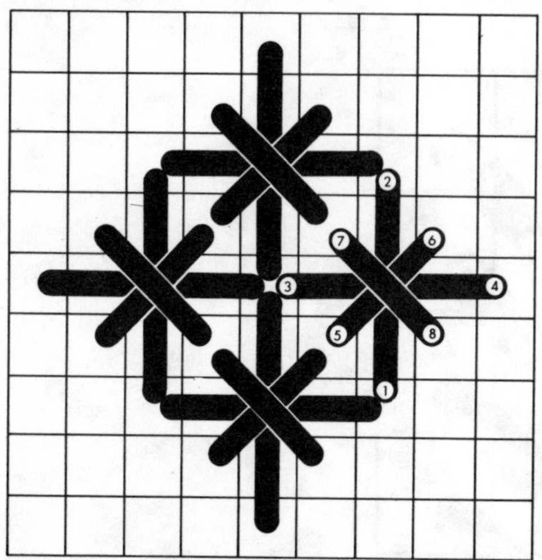


LEFT-HANDED STITCHERS

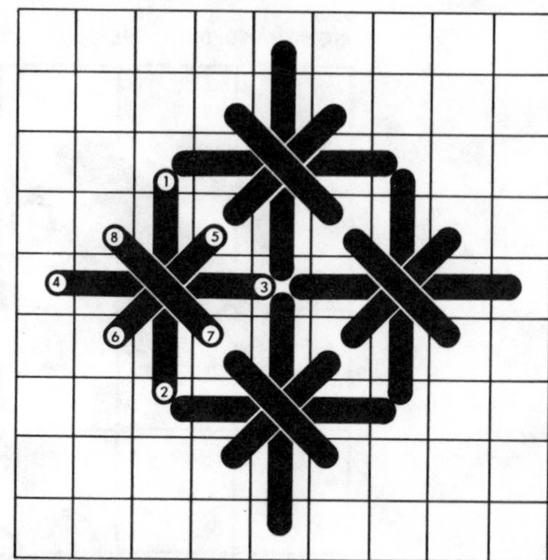


The diamond shape left in each letter will fit four Double Straight Cross units. Make sure that you cross each unit in the same direction, or your work will look sloppy.

## DIAMOND EYELET

The diamond shape also fits one Diamond Eyelet unit, closely related to the Eyelet stitch shown on page 50. A double strand of yarn must be used on 14-ct. canvas. Work from the outside of the unit down into the center ("C"). You may find it convenient to turn the canvas as you stitch around the unit. Make sure the last stitch is securely fastened off on the back of the canvas, or it will look lumpy.

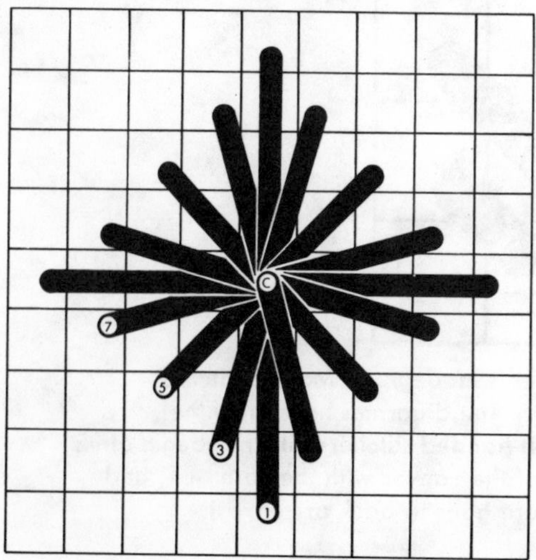

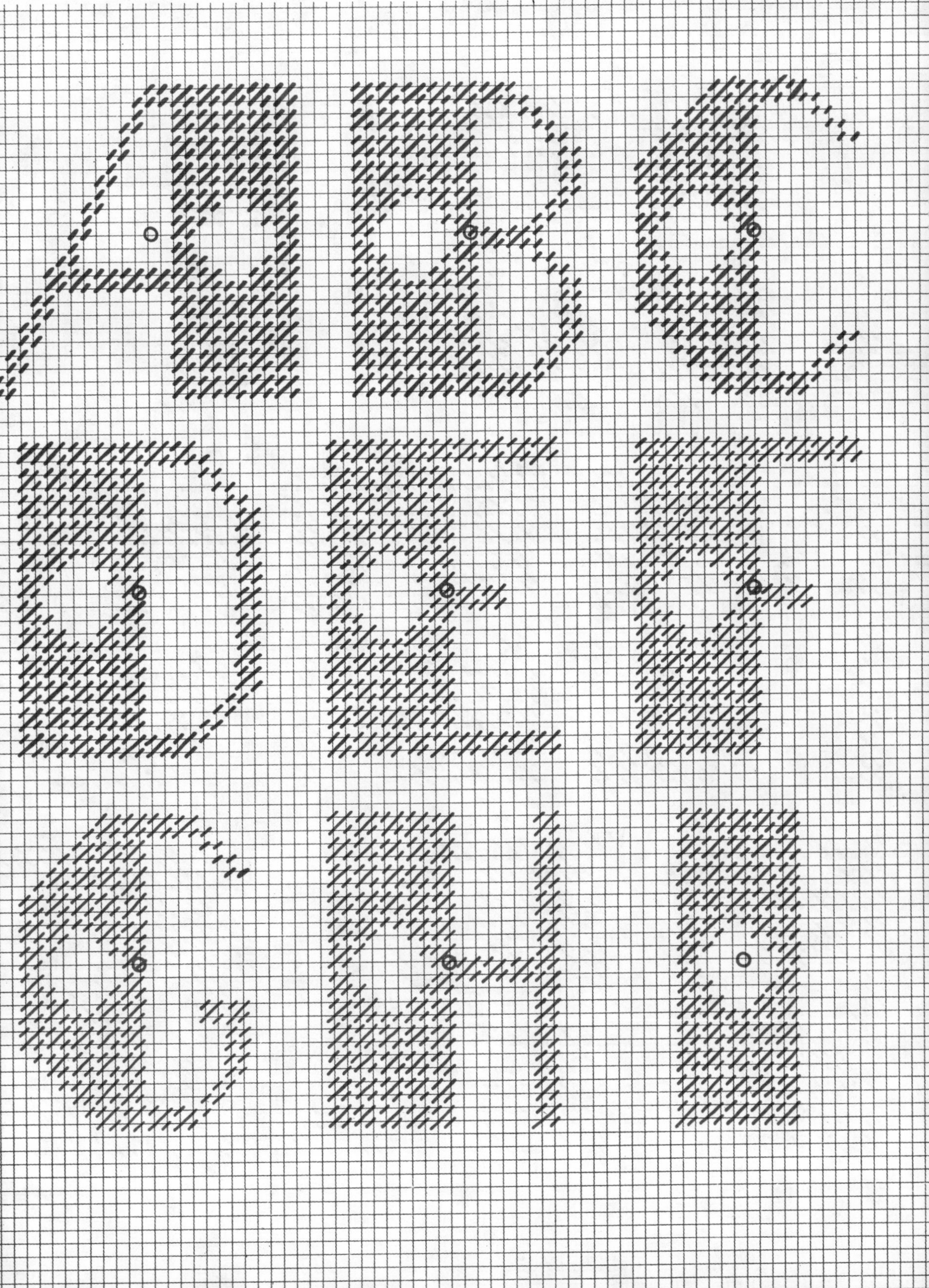

# CLASSIC

**Double strand on 14-ct. canvas**
**height: 15 threads**

This simple, elegant alphabet style is excellent for names and initials. It is based on the Oblique, or Slanting Gobelin stitch, diagramed here for your convenience.

A color picture using Classic appears on page viii.

## OBLIQUE GOBELIN

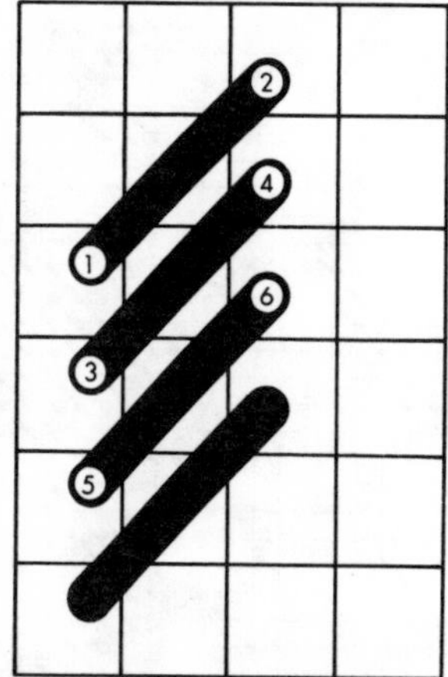


The letters of this alphabet are based on the Oblique, or Slanting Gobelin stitch, shown here worked vertically.

# OLD WESTERN

**Double strand on 14-ct. canvas**
**height: 9 threads**

This is another alphabet based on poster letters, with the flavor of the Old West. The letters are small and very useful for making up words.

The letters use the Flat stitch (page 72) in an elongated form.

A color picture using Old Western appears on page v.

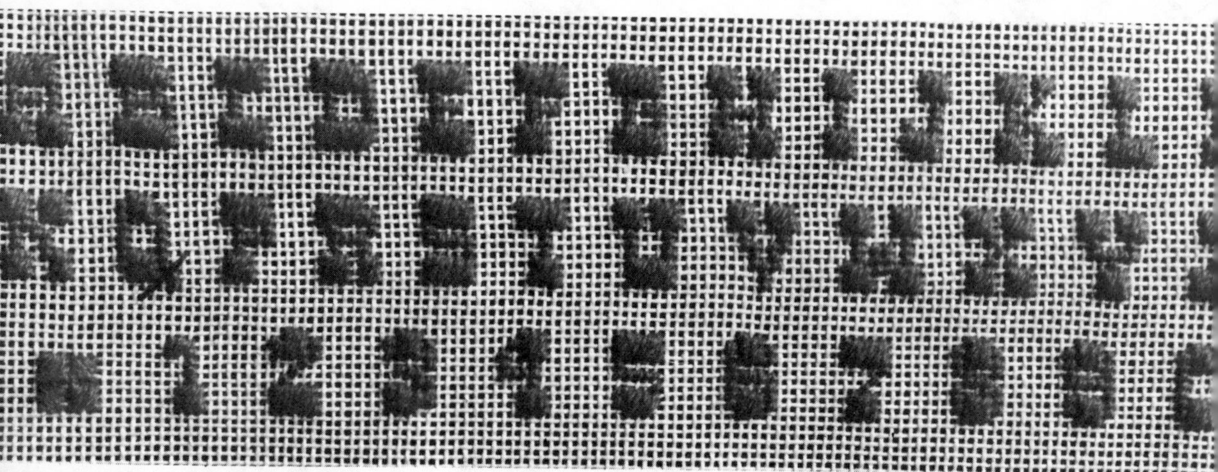

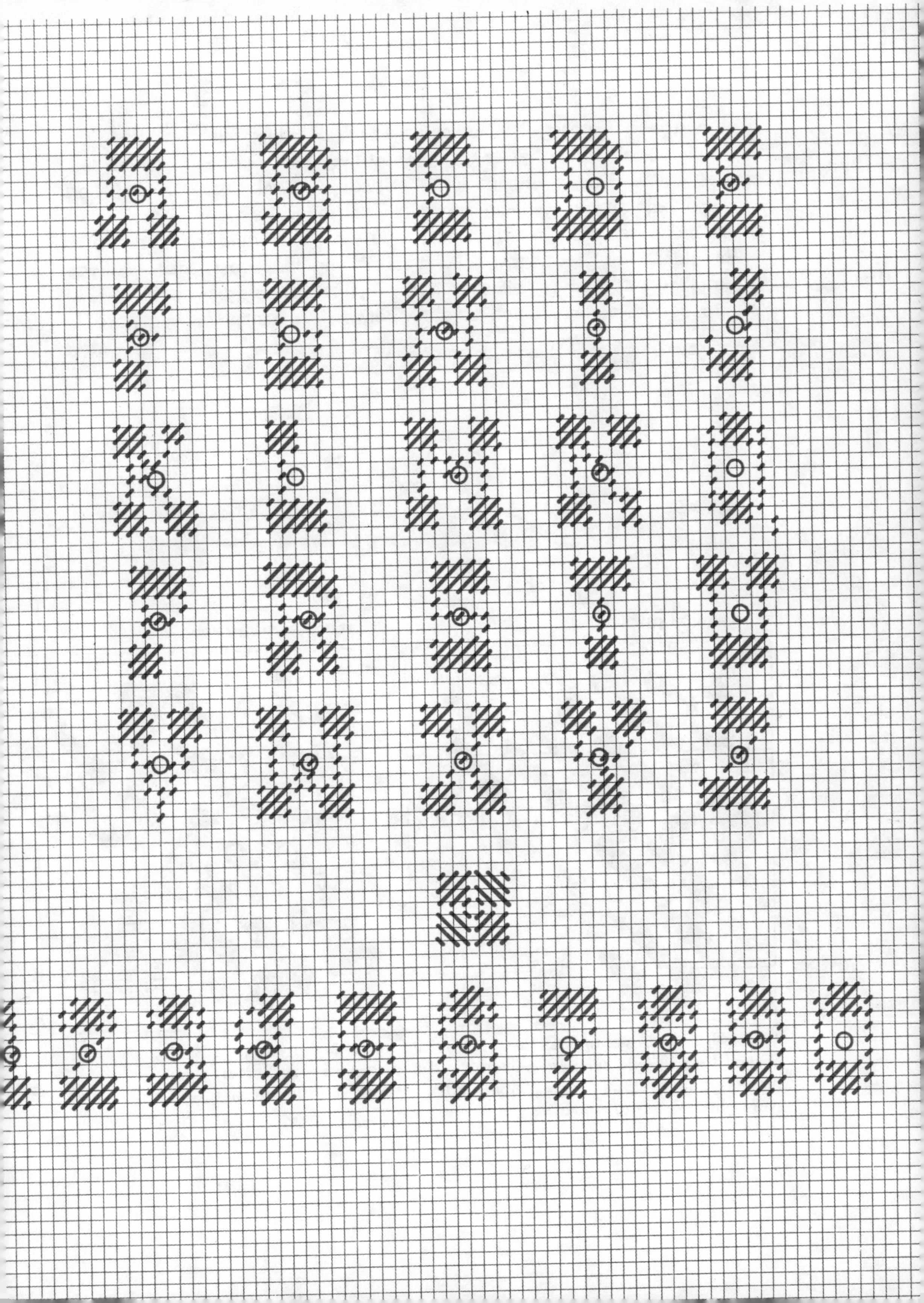

# TYPEWRITER PRINT

**Double strand on 14-ct. canvas**
**height: 21 threads, base average**

Here is a whole alphabet in lower case with a contemporary feeling. It is made up of units of Flat stitch, diagramed here with right-handed and left-handed counts. You will notice that the location of the center of the letters varies so that you can use them individually. If used to form a word, the letters should be aligned along a straight line, and the centers should be ignored.

This alphabet is particularly tricky to space, and it is recommended that you diagram the letters before stitching them on canvas. You should have at least 24 threads between words and just a few between each letter within a word.

Typewriter Print is shown in color on page viii.

## FLAT STITCH

RIGHT-HANDED STITCHERS

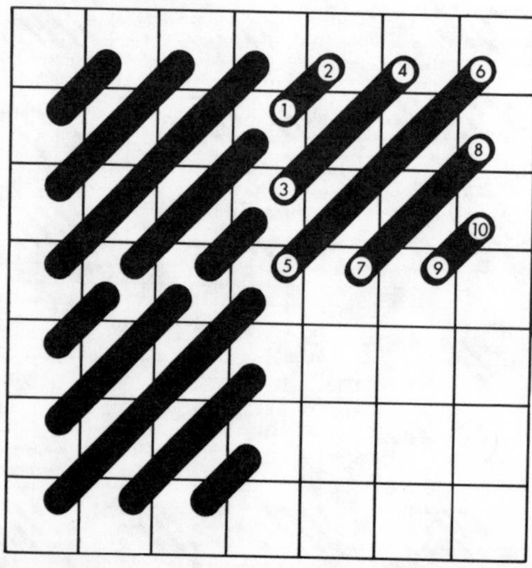


LEFT-HANDED STITCHERS

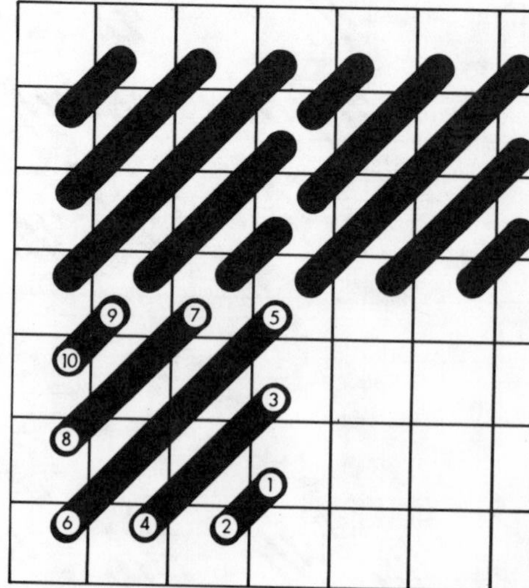


**This alphabet is based on the Flat stitch, which forms little blocks over 3 canvas threads. Odd numbers indicate the start of a stitch (yarn comes through to surface), and even numbers indicate the finish of the stitch (yarn goes to back of canvas).**

a b c d e f g
h i j k l m n
o p q r s t u
v w x y z ? $
1 2 3 4 5
6 7 8 9 0

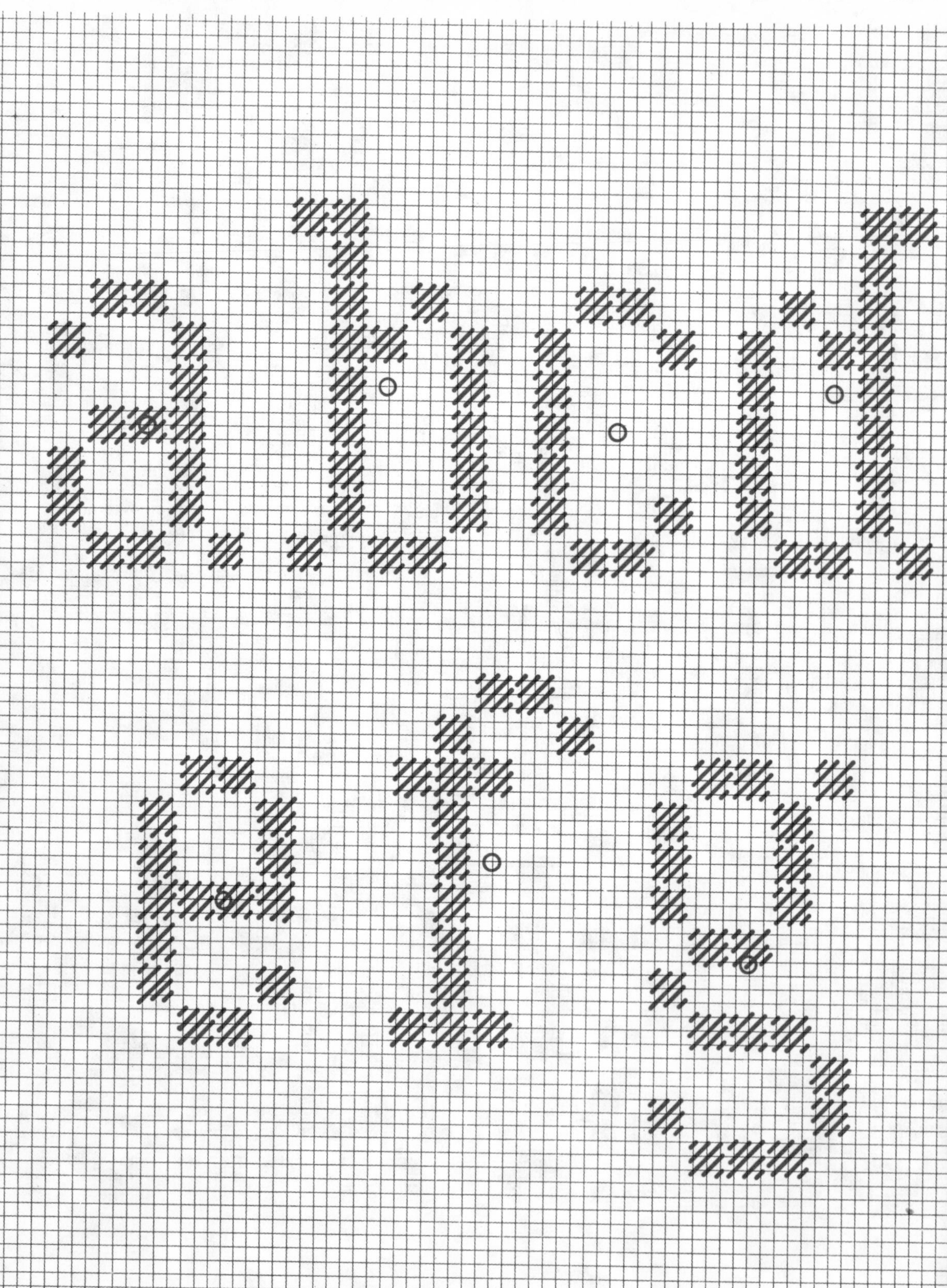

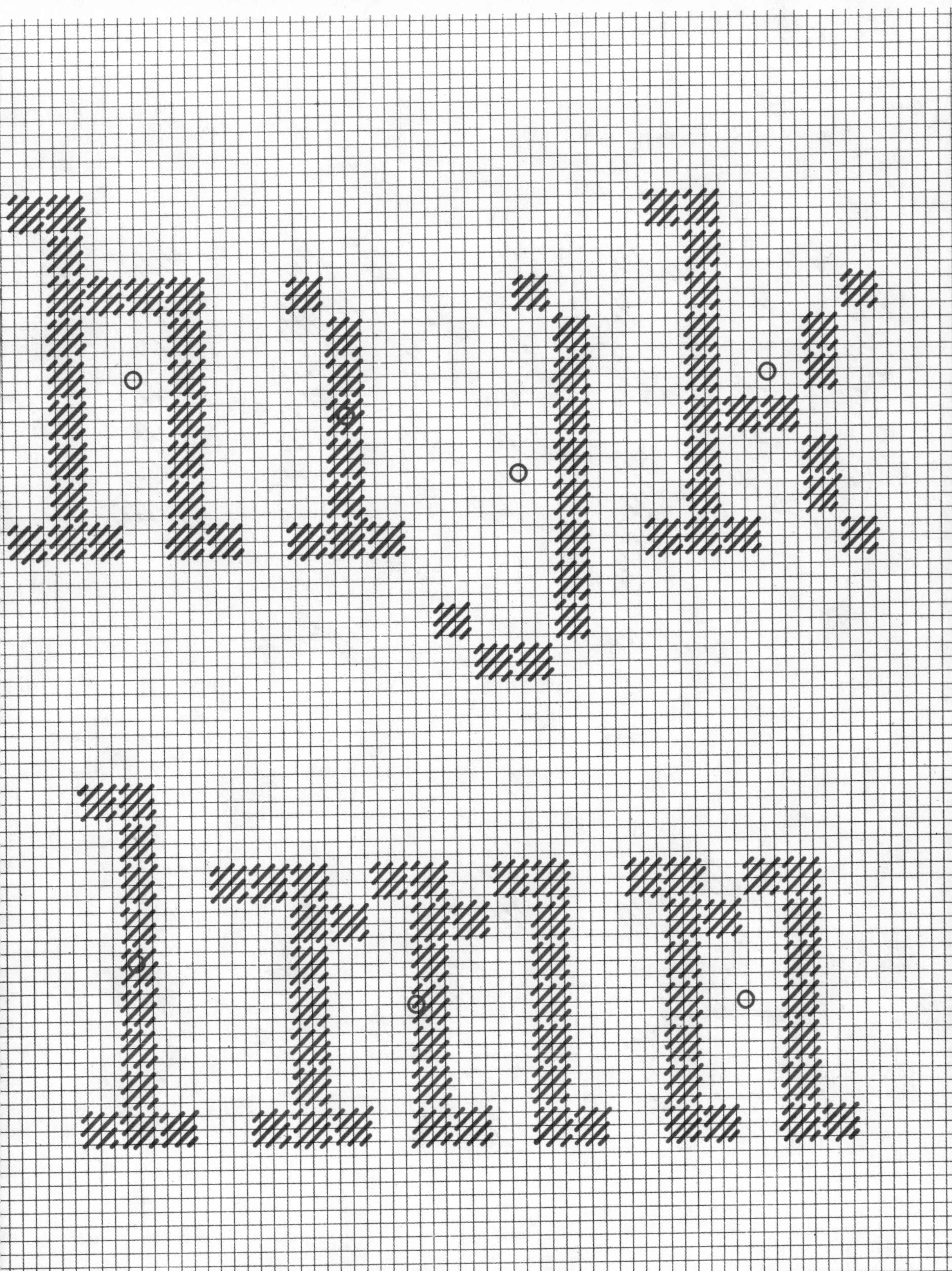

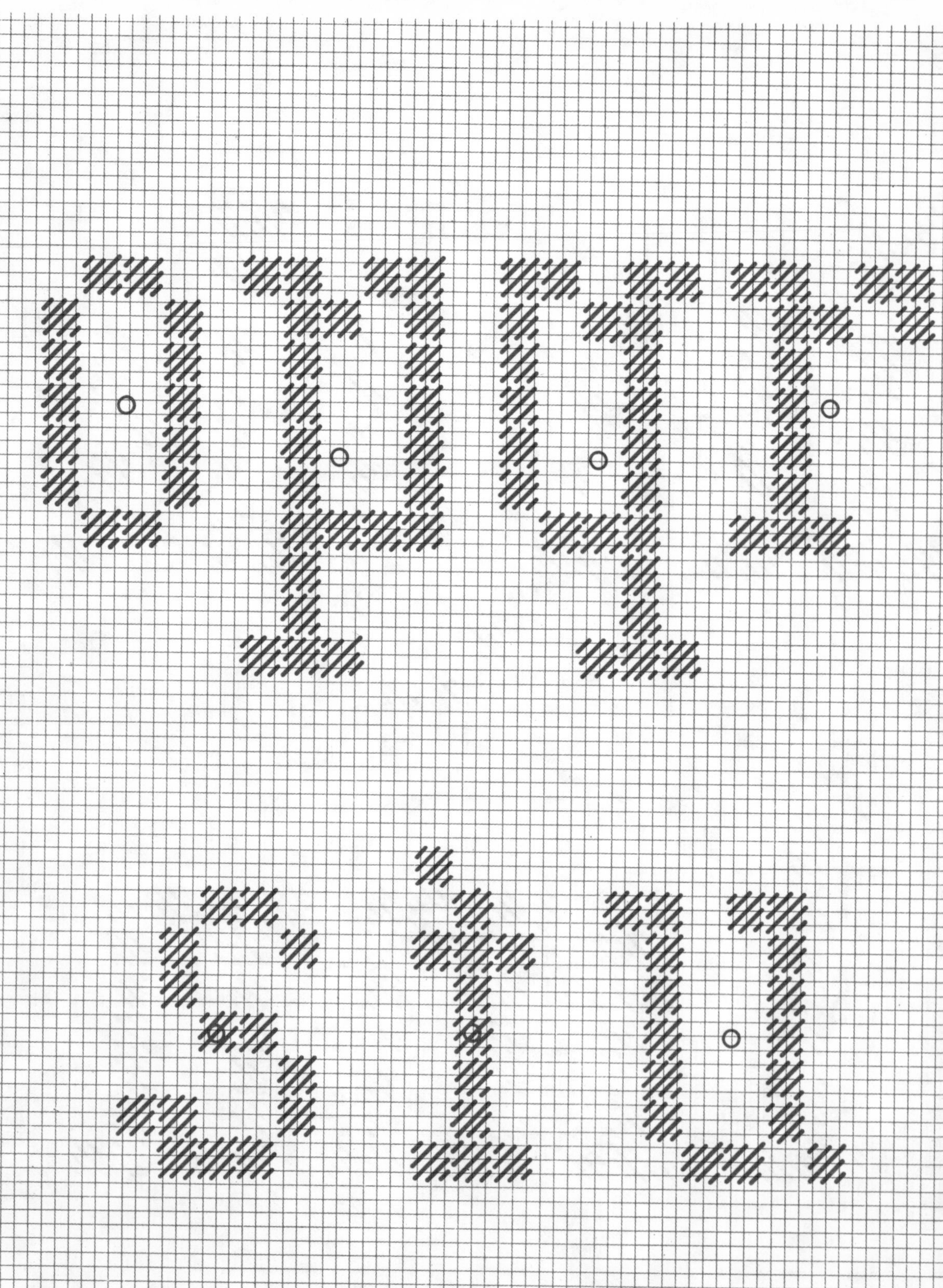

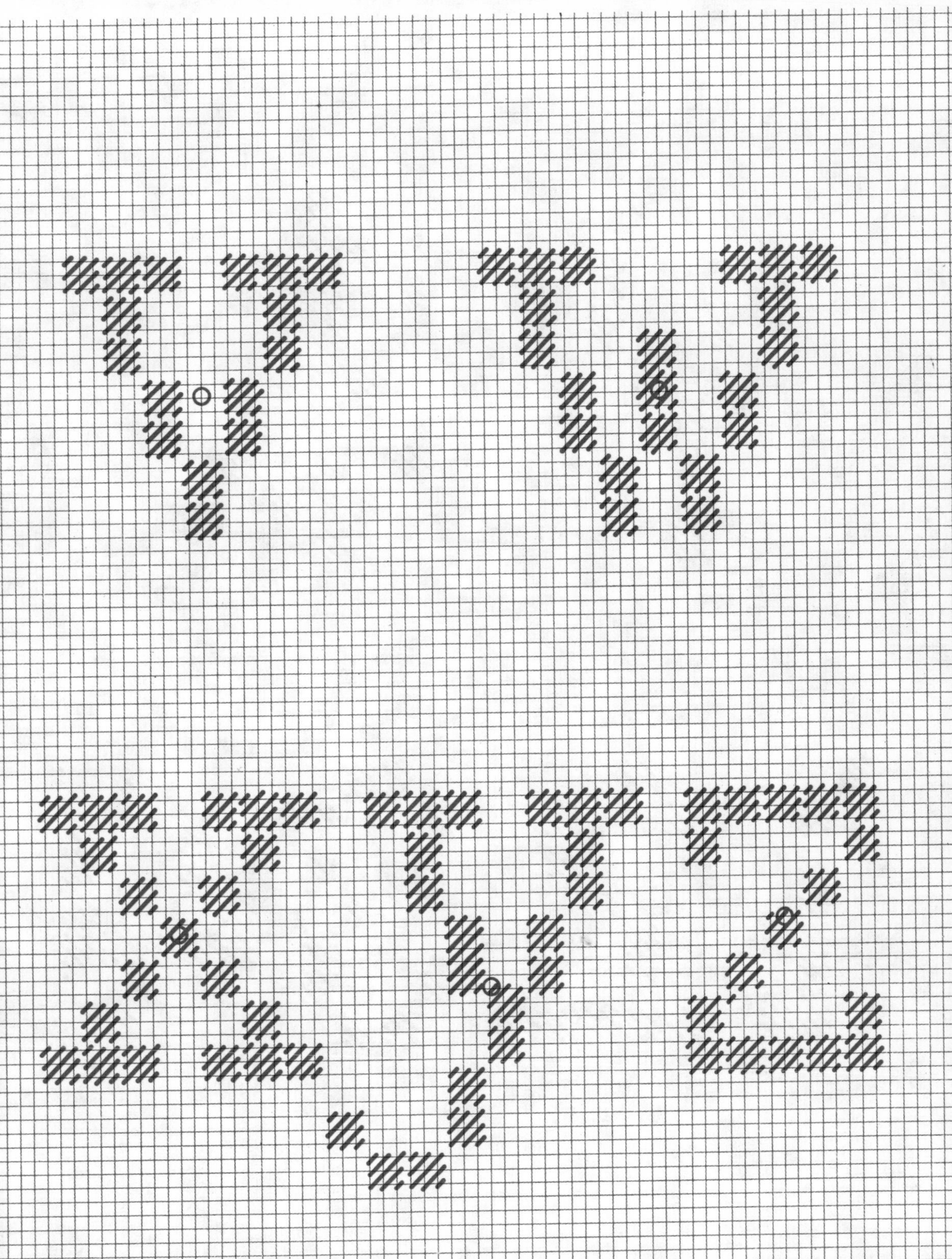

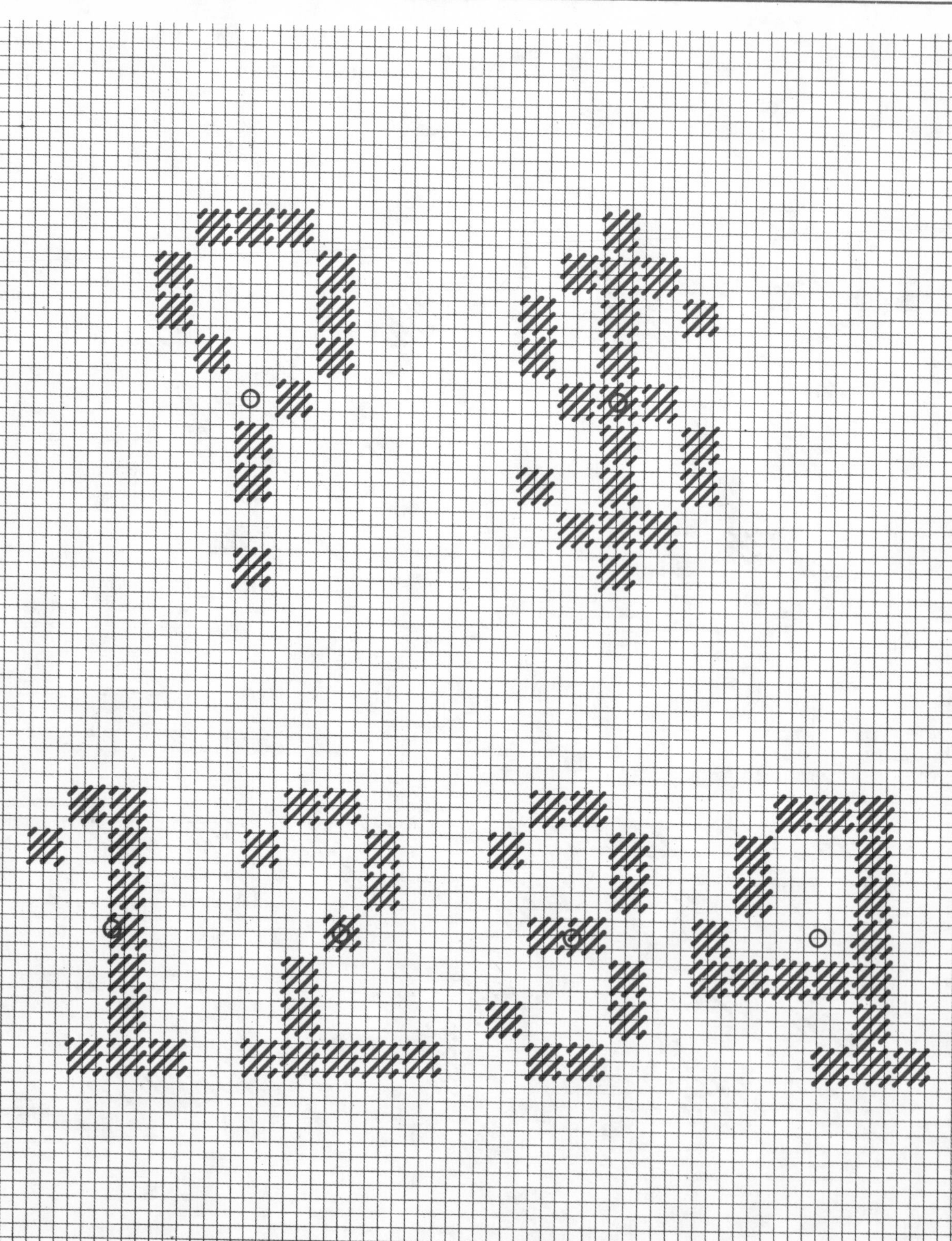

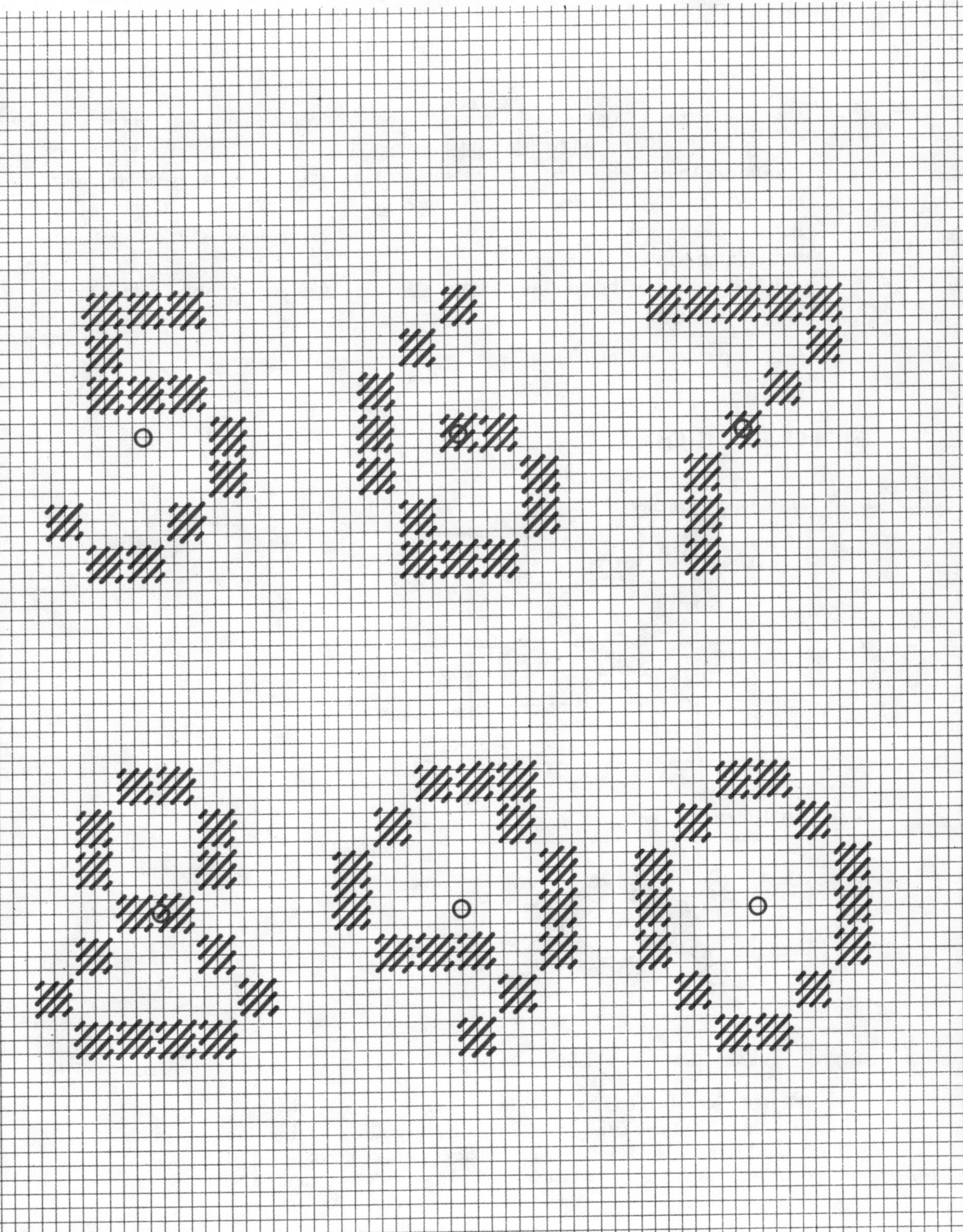

# CHINESE CROSS

**Double or full strand on 14-ct. canvas**
**height: 10 threads**

Chinese Cross is made up of Cross Stitches, diagramed here with the counts for right-handed and left-handed stitchers. You will have to experiment with the thickness of yarn you are using to see that the canvas is being adequately covered. Start with a double strand in a corner of your work. If this looks skimpy, work with a full strand; it is unattractive to have canvas peeking through the finished work.

Note, also, that the centers of these letters fall over canvas holes rather than canvas thread intersections.

A color picture using Chinese Cross letters appears on page viii.

## CROSS STITCH

RIGHT-HANDED STITCHERS

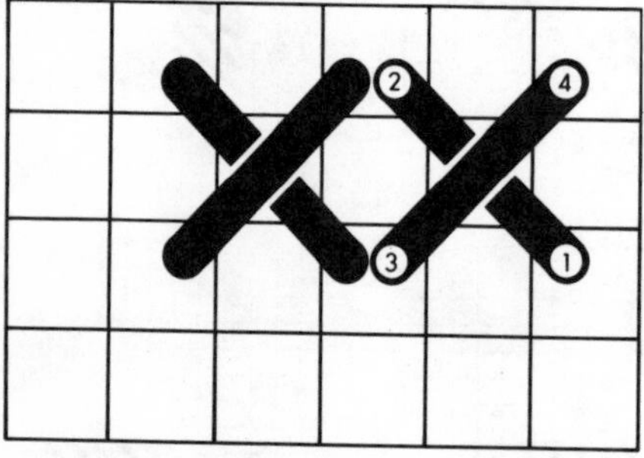


LEFT-HANDED STITCHERS

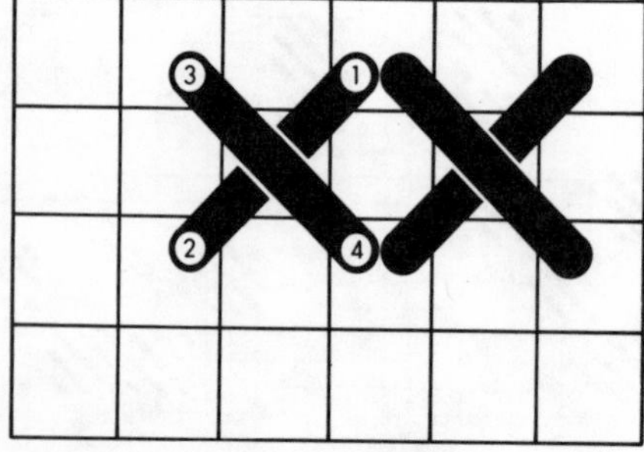


This alphabet is based on the long-lived Cross Stitch, diagramed here for right-handed and left-handed stitchers. Make sure all stitches are crossed in the same direction. You may have to experiment with a double or full strand on 14-ct. canvas to see which covers adequately.

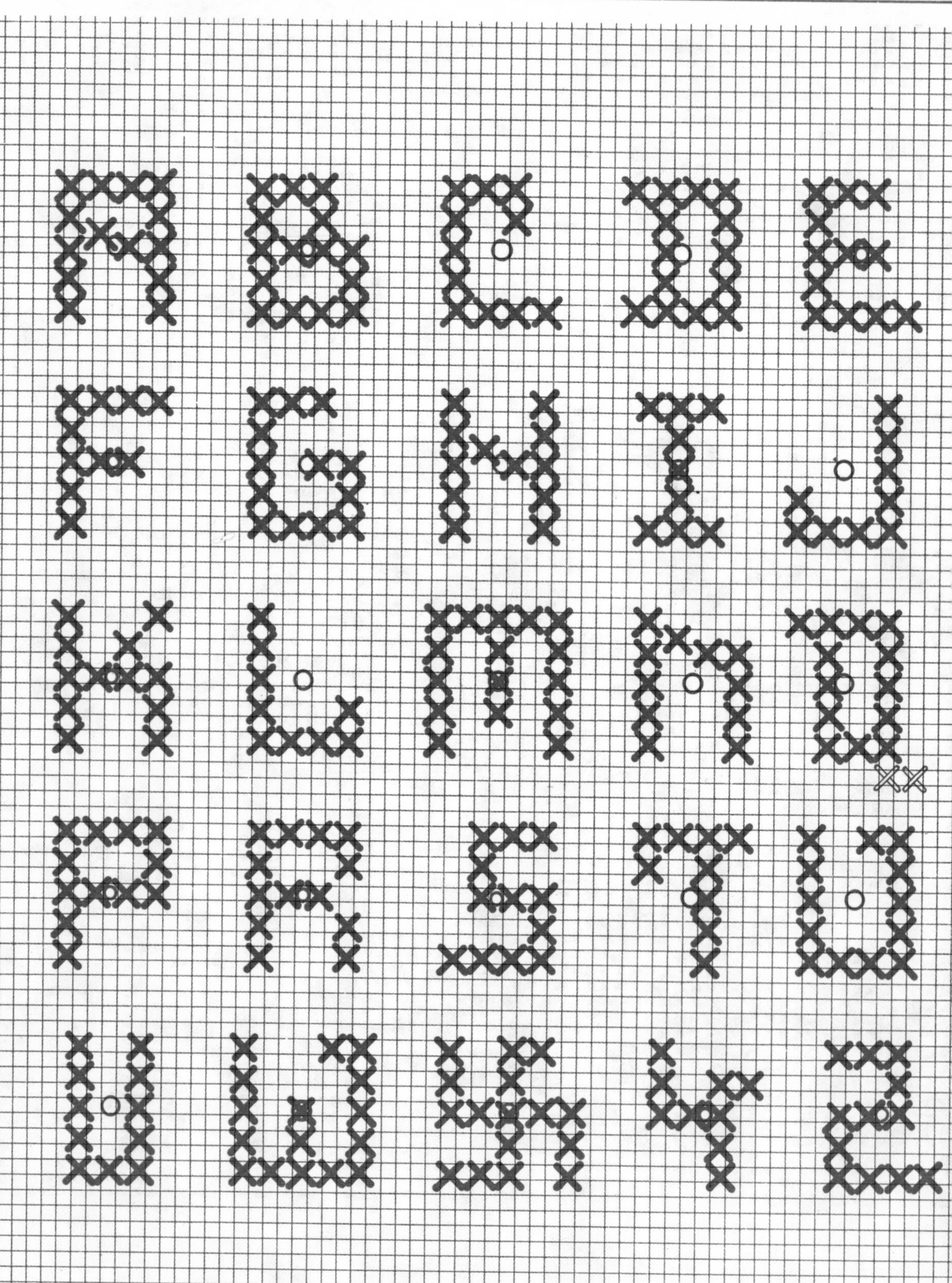

# CARNIVAL

**Double strand on 14-ct. canvas**
**height: 19 threads**

Carnival is based on the lettering found in circus posters and looks very nice stitched in brightly contrasting colors. Stitch the outline first and then fill in the letter with a second color. The Cross Stitch that appears at the sides of the letters can be substituted with French Knots, a stitch used in crewel and surface embroidery.

A project using Carnival letters is shown in color on page viii.

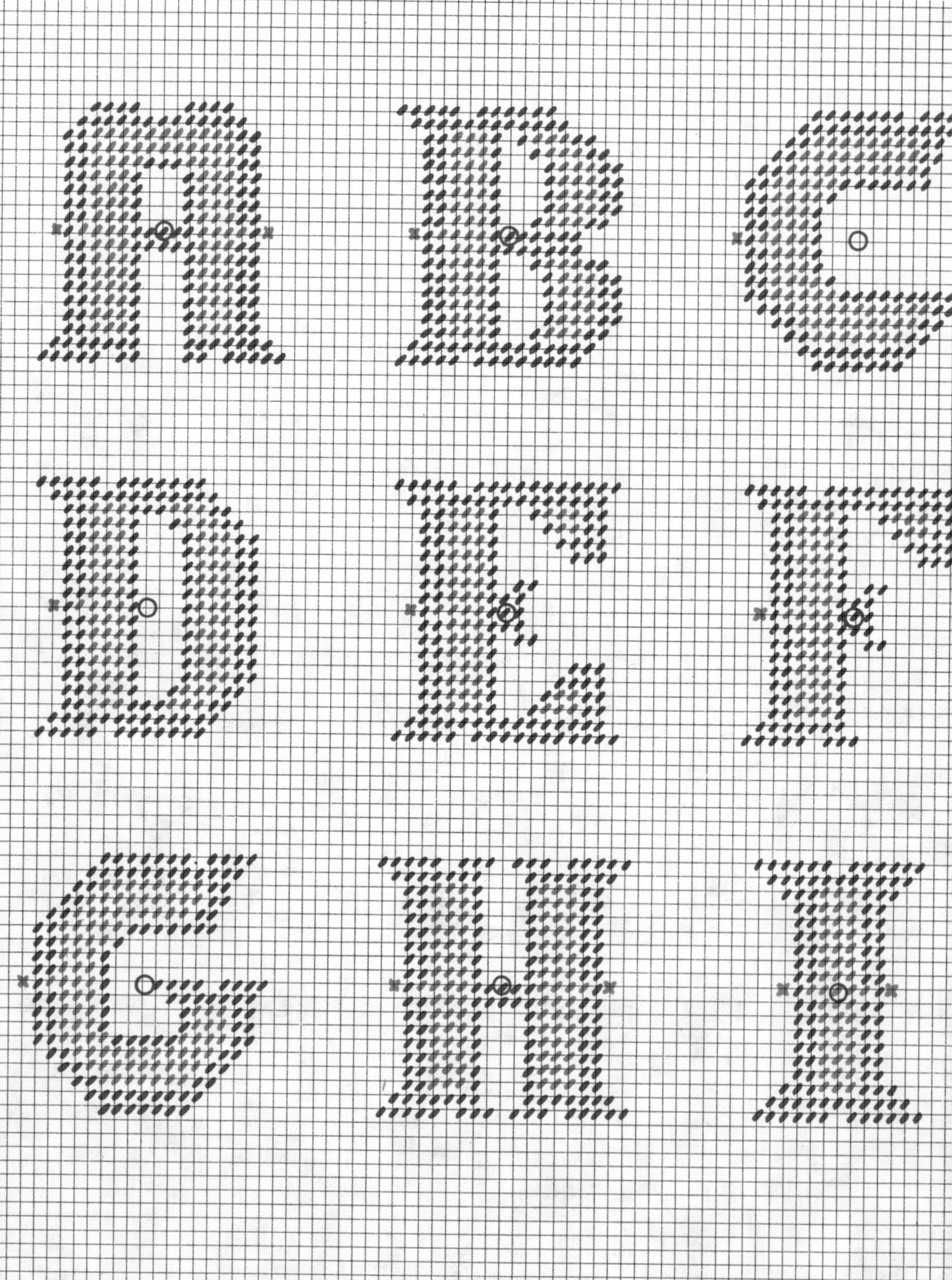

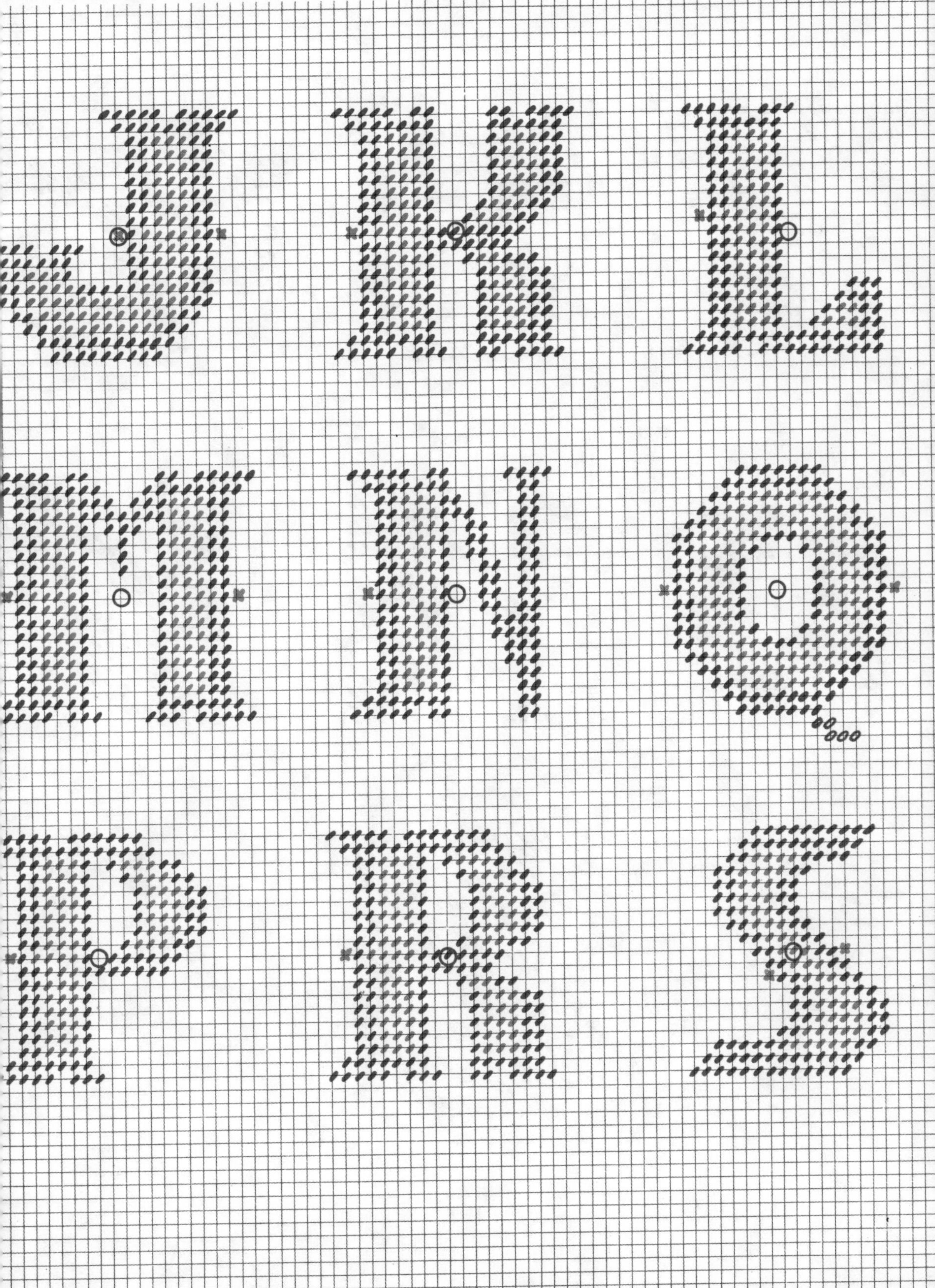

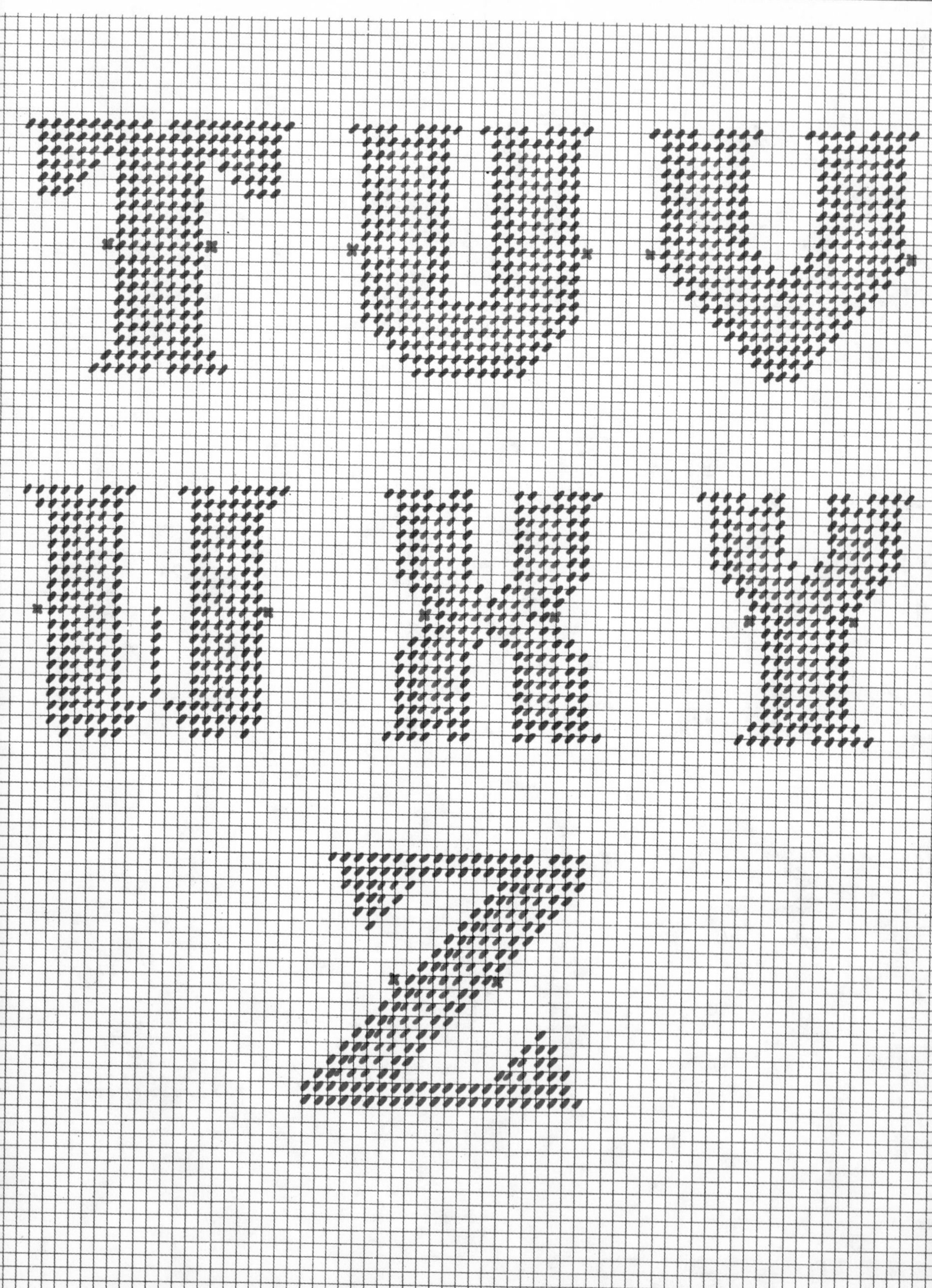

# THUNDERBIRD

**Full strand on 14-ct. canvas**
**height: 21 threads**

The bold look of these letters is reminiscent of Indian hieroglyphs and is particularly pleasing to men. The alphabet must be used in a project that will not receive much hard wear, as the stitches are quite long and are susceptible to snagging and pilling. Note that the centers of the letters fall over canvas holes rather than intersections. Also, make sure that horizontal and vertical stitches share holes, or canvas will show through the finished work.

The picture on the following page shows a Thunderbird "S" initial in a coaster under glass.

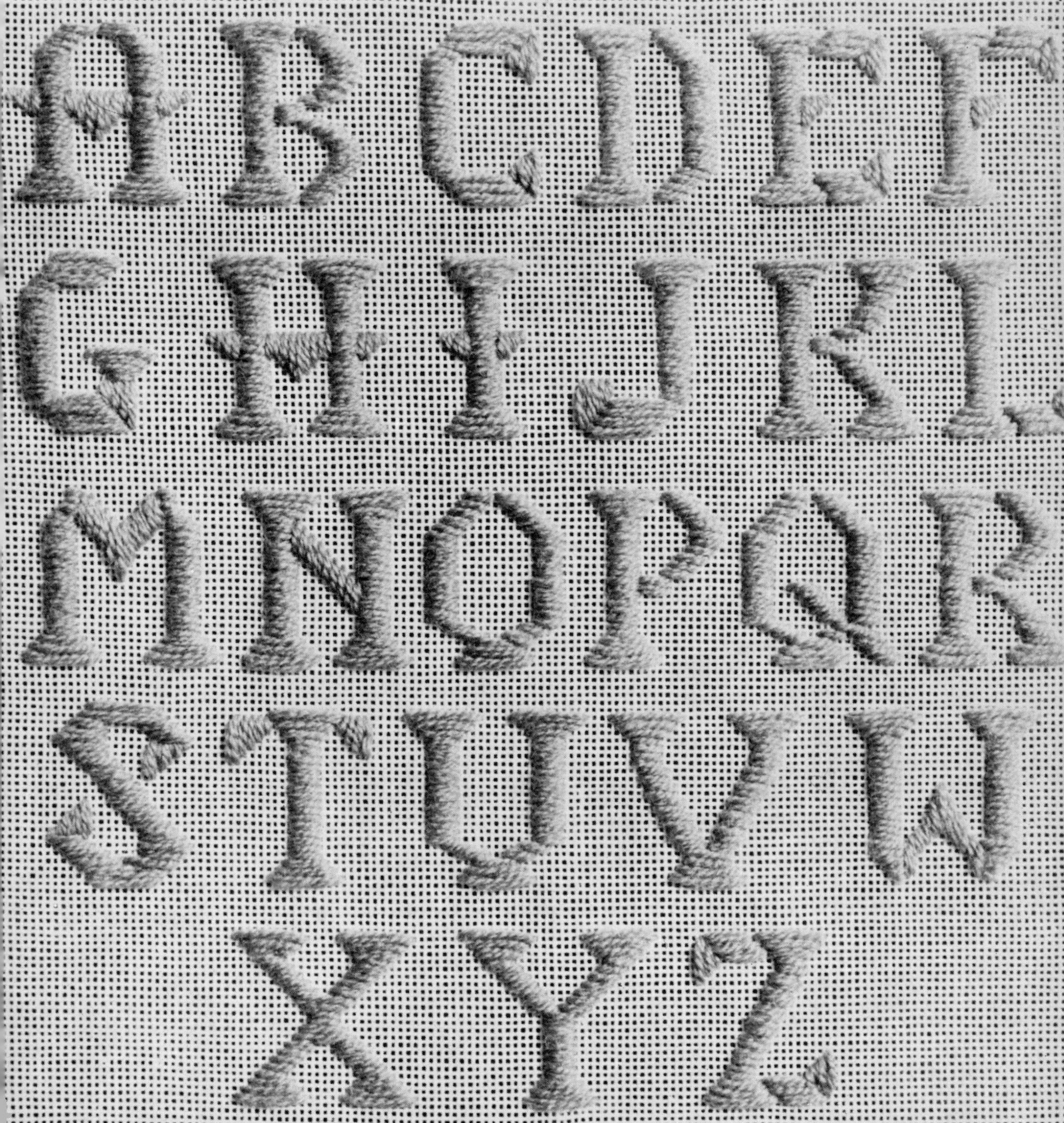

## GOBELIN DROIT

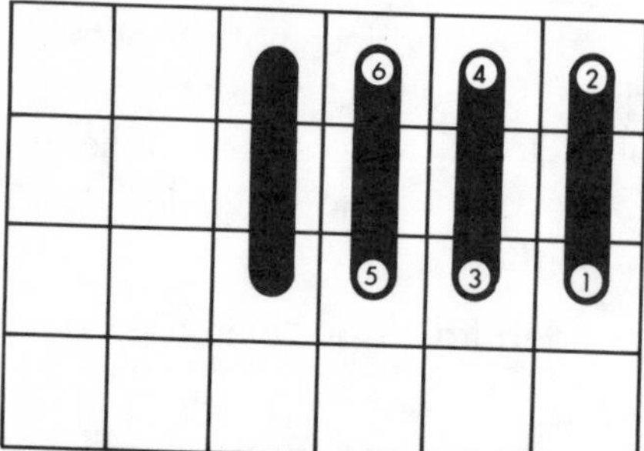


Thunderbird is made up of varying lengths of Gobelin Droit stitch, which is a straight stitch. There should be a single canvas thread between stitches; if you skip another, canvas will show through the work. Also, make sure that Gobelin stitches coming together at right angles meet in the same holes, or canvas will show through.

The initial "S" is centered in a Basketweave background, with a border of Flat stitch (page 72). The Flat stitch units are outlined with a single row of Tent in metallic thread for further decoration, and the piece is mounted in a frame under glass to be used as a coaster or, possibly, a mini-picture.

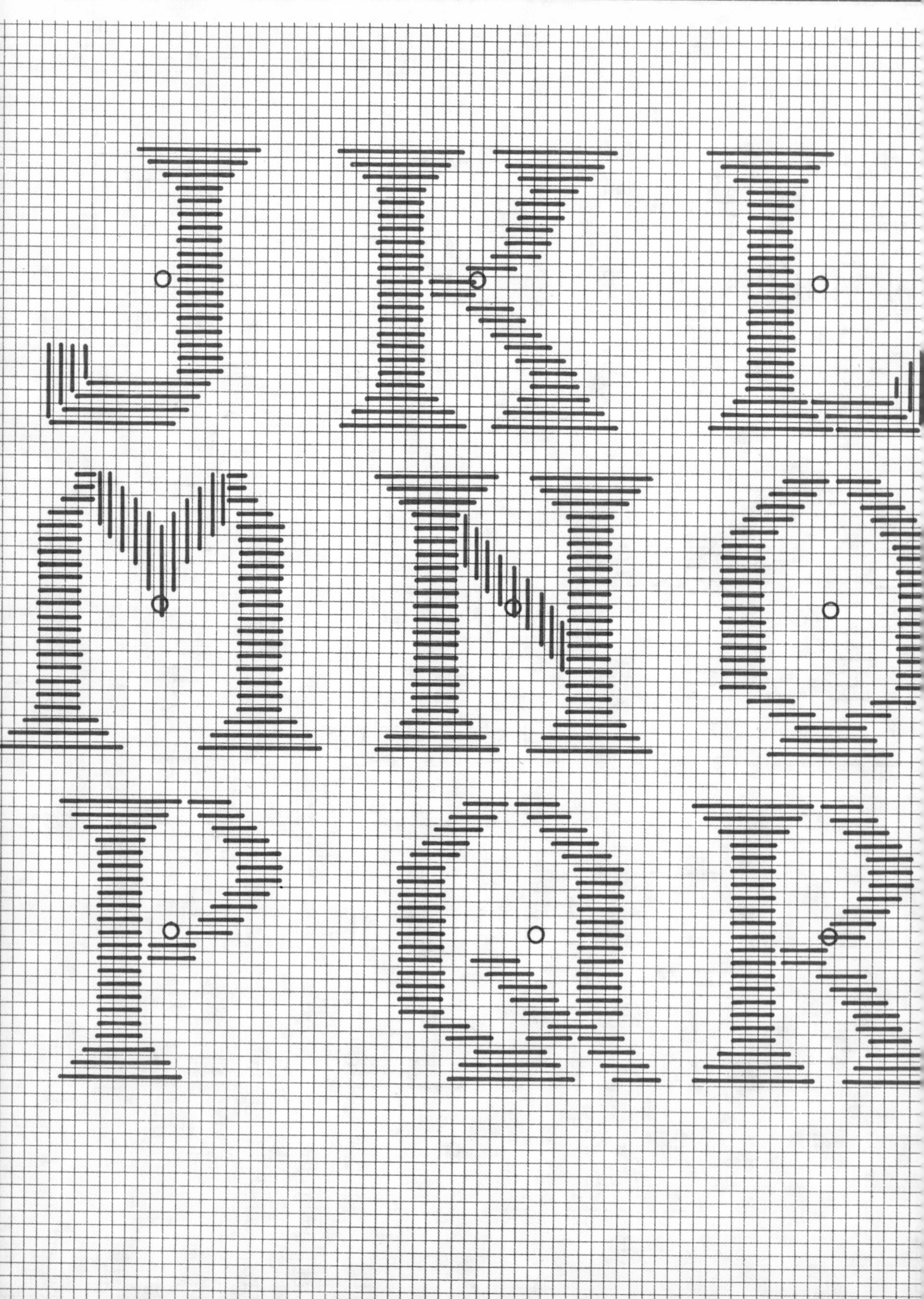

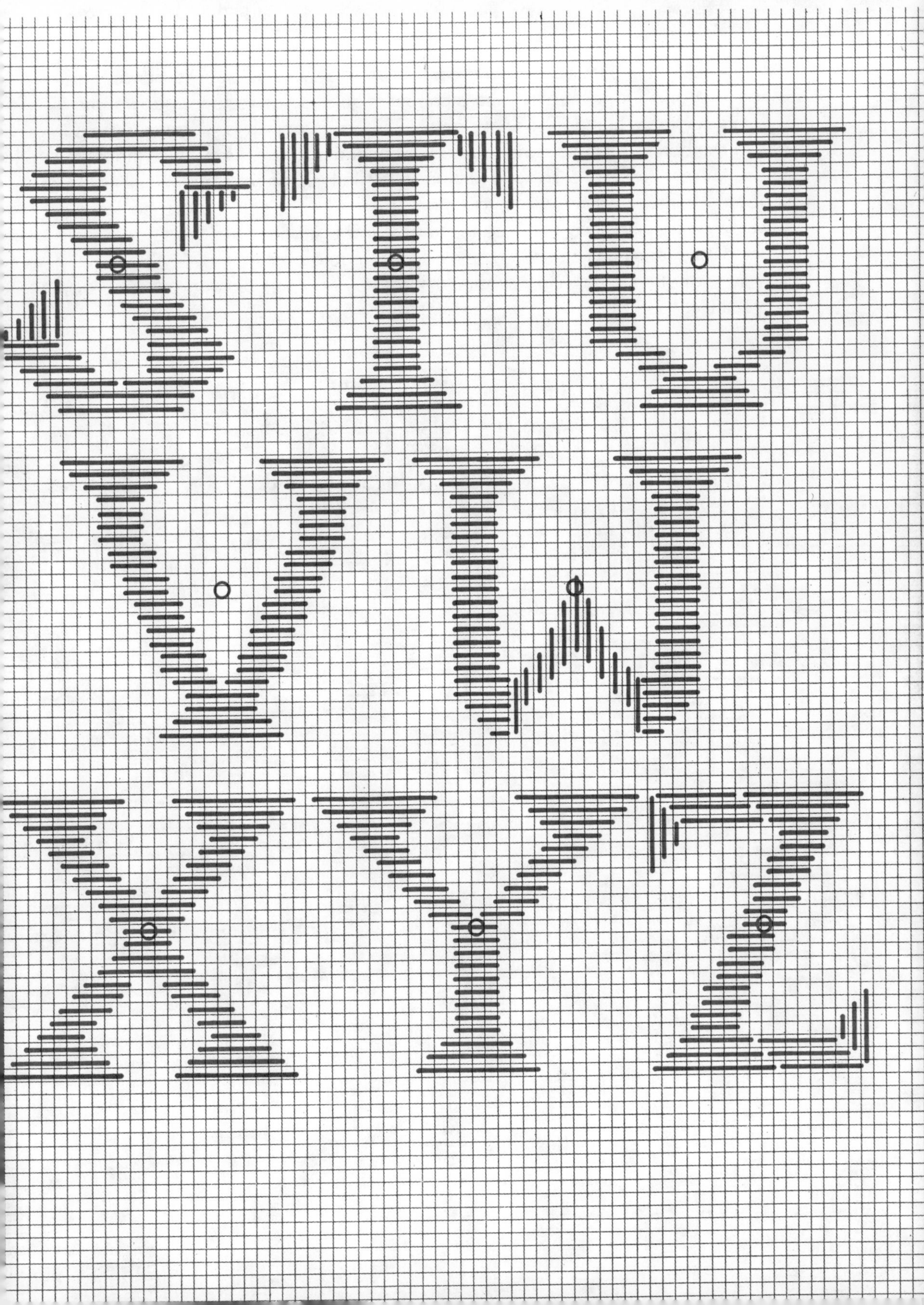

# SMYRNA

**Full strand on 14-ct. canvas**
**height: 20 threads**

The block letters of this alphabet are made up of Smyrna stitch units; hence, the name. Worked in two colors, the alphabet is quite bold. To tone it down, the letters can be worked in a single color. The Smyrna stitch is diagramed here with numbering for right-handed and left-handed stitchers. Make sure that the top unit crosses in the same direction in all letters, or your work will look sloppy. When working with two colors, the "X" units can be stitched for a whole letter, and then the second color can be introduced. If one color is being used, each unit can be completed as you go along.

For variation, you might substitute Crossed Corners, diagramed here, or Eyelet (Algerian Eye) shown on page 50 for the Smyrna units.

A color picture showing Smyrna appears on page viii.

RIGHT-HANDED STITCHERS

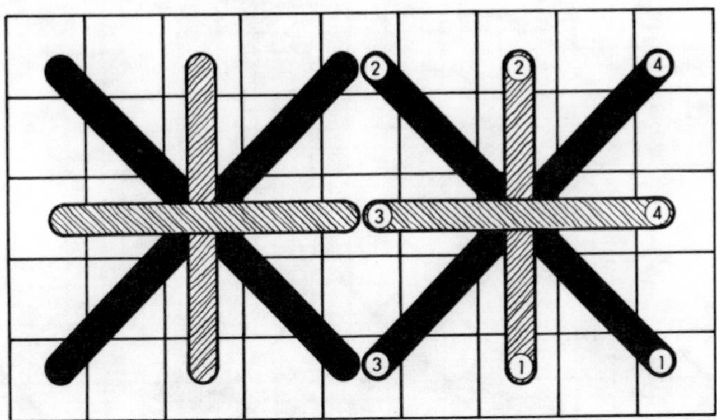

LEFT-HANDED STITCHERS

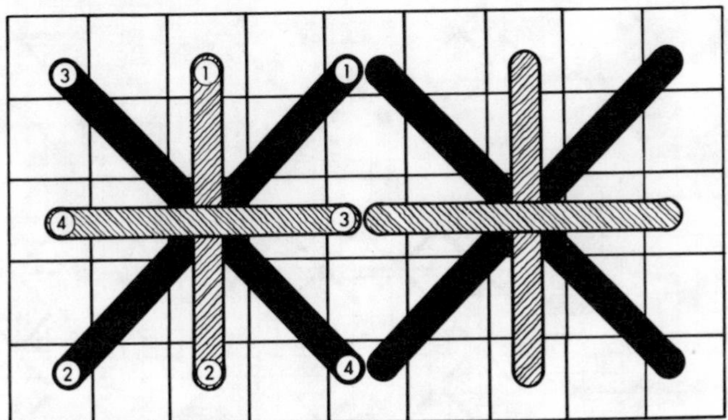

The Smyrna unit is composed of an "X" with an upright cross superimposed on top. As with all crossed stitches, it is important to the finished look of the work that you cross each stitch in the same direction. Use a full strand of yarn for both crosses.

RIGHT-HANDED STITCHERS

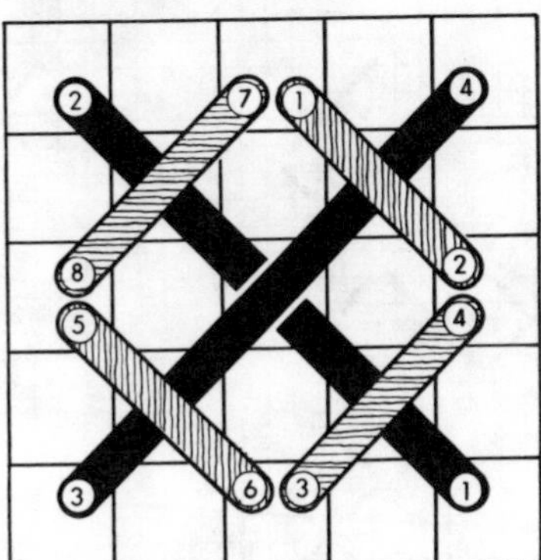

LEFT-HANDED STITCHERS

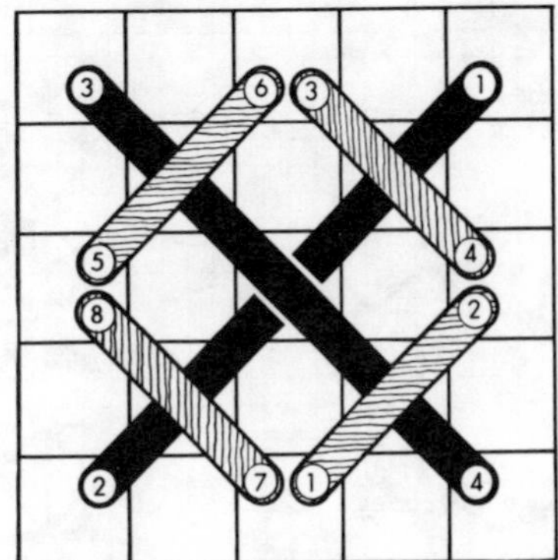

The Smyrna stitch can be substituted with Crossed Corners, or Rice, stitch, which is a favorite with many needlepointers. The "X" is stitched first in one color in a full strand (on 14-ct. canvas), and then each corner is tied down with a double strand in a second color.

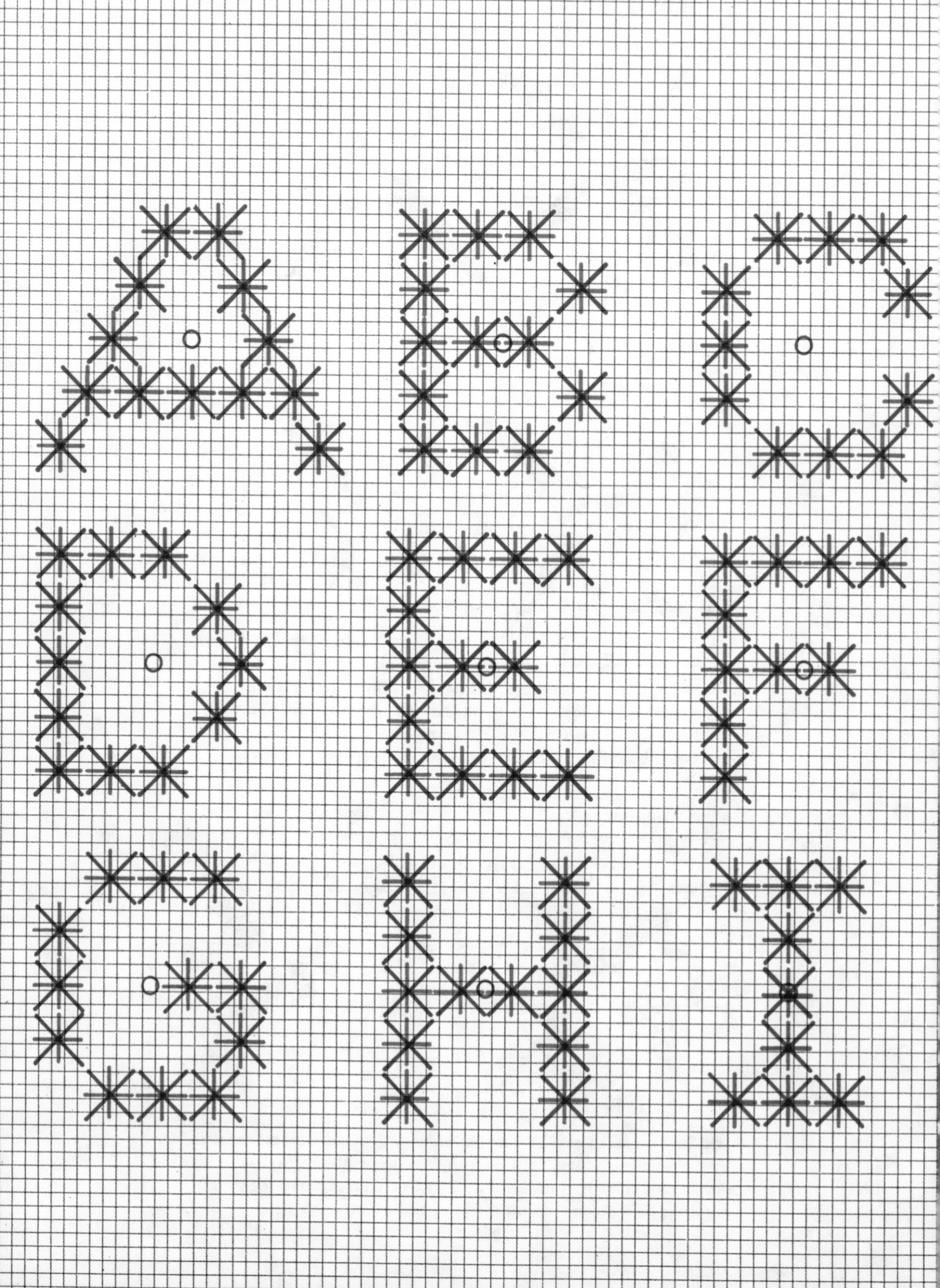

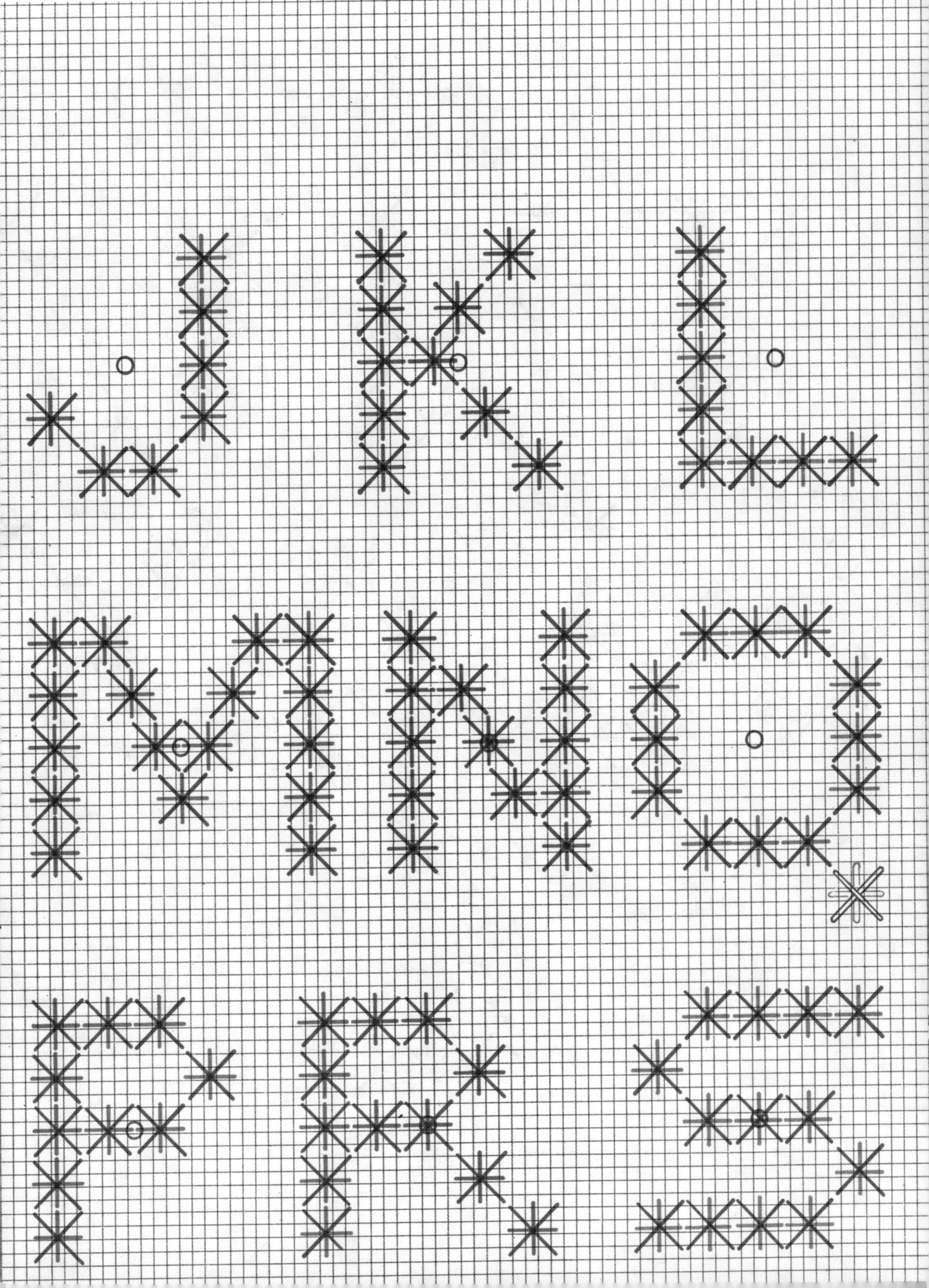

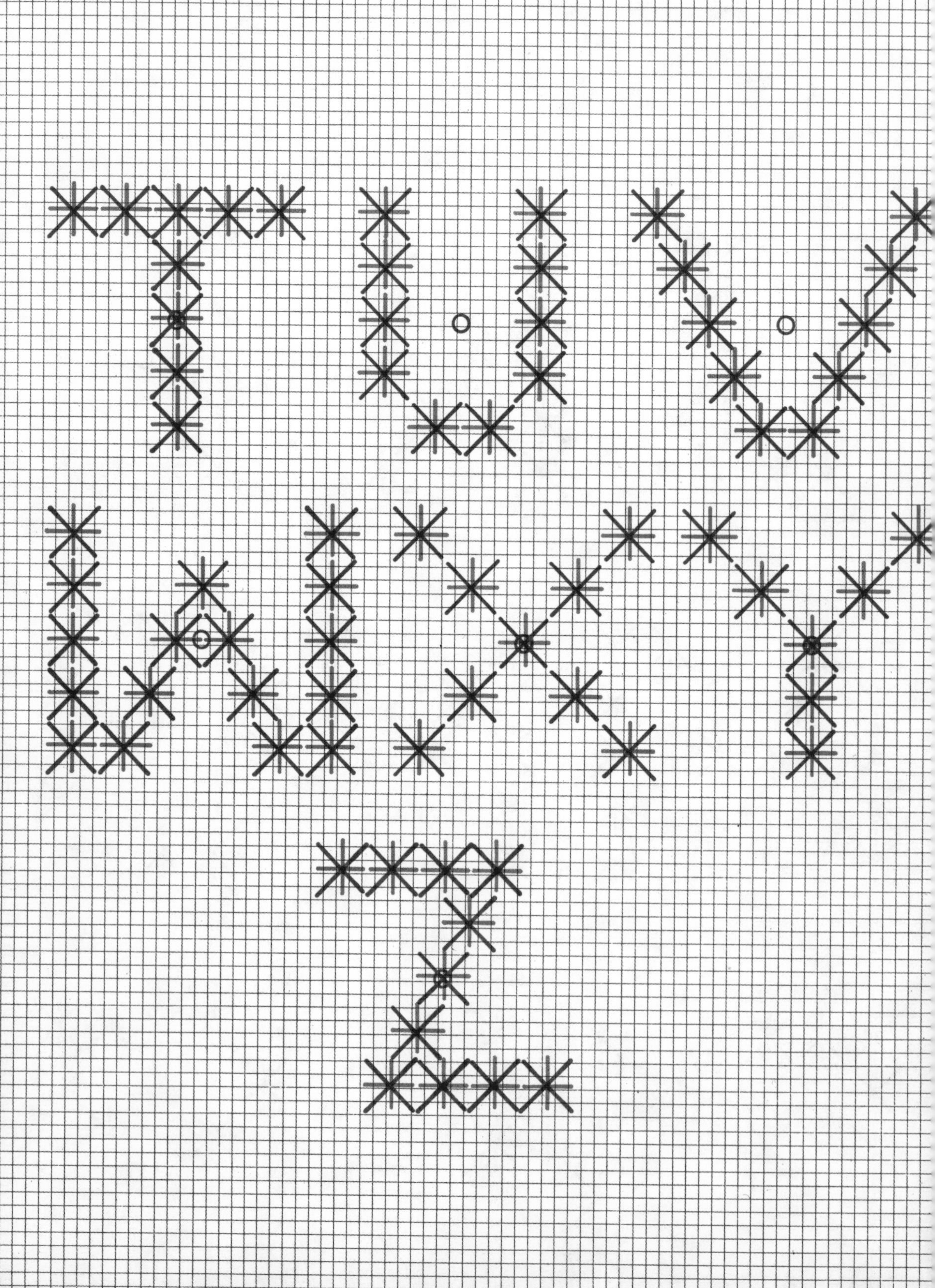

# CHINESE TERRESTRIAL SIGNS

**Double strand on 14-ct. canvas**
**height: 20 threads, base average**

These graceful symbols have various interpretations. They represent years in twelve-year cycles in Chinese lore. The years are analogous to our zodiac signs. A single Sign, representing a friend's birth sign, can be used in a small, personal gift, such as the one shown on page 100. Note that the symbol has been beaded rather than stitched. Instead of making a Tent stitch, slip a bead onto a thin needle and cross a canvas intersection as you would with yarn.

A color picture using a Chinese Terrestrial Sign appears on page iii.

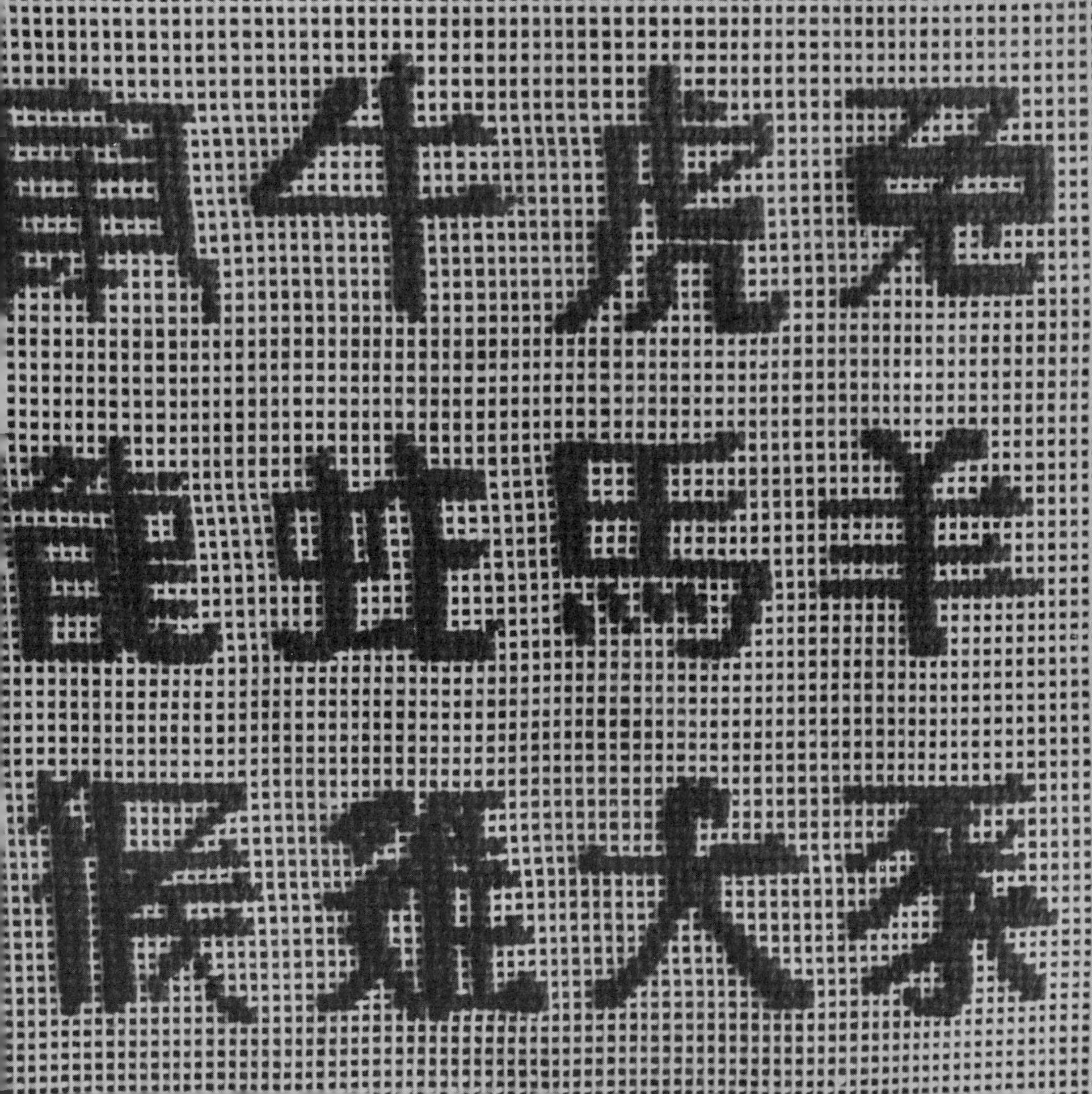

1. Year of the Rat (1900, '12, '24, '36, '48, '60, '72, '84)
*Aries* (March 21 to April 20)

2. Year of the Ox (1901, '13, '25, '37, '49, '61, '73, '85)
*Taurus* (April 21 to May 21)

3. Year of the Tiger (1902, '14, '26, '38, '50, '62, '74, '86)
*Gemini* (May 22 to June 21)

4. Year of the Hare (1903, '15, '27, '39, '51, '63, '75, '87) Moon Children
*Cancer* (June 22 to July 23)

5. Year of the Dragon (1904, '16, '28, '40, '52, '64, '76, '88)
*Leo* (July 24 to August 23)

6. Year of the Serpent (1905, '17, '29, '41, '53, '65, '77, '89)
*Virgo* (August 24 to September 23)

7. Year of the Horse (1906, '18, '30, '42, '54, '66, '78, '90)
*Libra* (September 24 to October 23)

8. Year of the Goat (1907, '19, '31, '43, '55, '67, '79, '91)
*Scorpio* (October 24 to November 22)

9. Year of the Monkey (1908, '20, '32, '44, '56, '68, '80, '92)
*Sagittarius* (November 23 to December 20)

10. Year of the Cock (1909, '21, '33, '45, '57, '69, '81, '93)
*Capricorn* (December 22 to January 20)

11. Year of the Dog (1910, '22, '34, '46, '58, '70, '82, '94)
*Aquarius* (January 21 to February 19)

12. Year of the Boar (1911, '23, '35, '47, '59, '71, '83, '95)
*Pisces* (February 20 to March 20)

Information found in *Outlines of Chinese Symbolism and Art Motives.* by C. A. S. Williams, Shanghai, 1932.

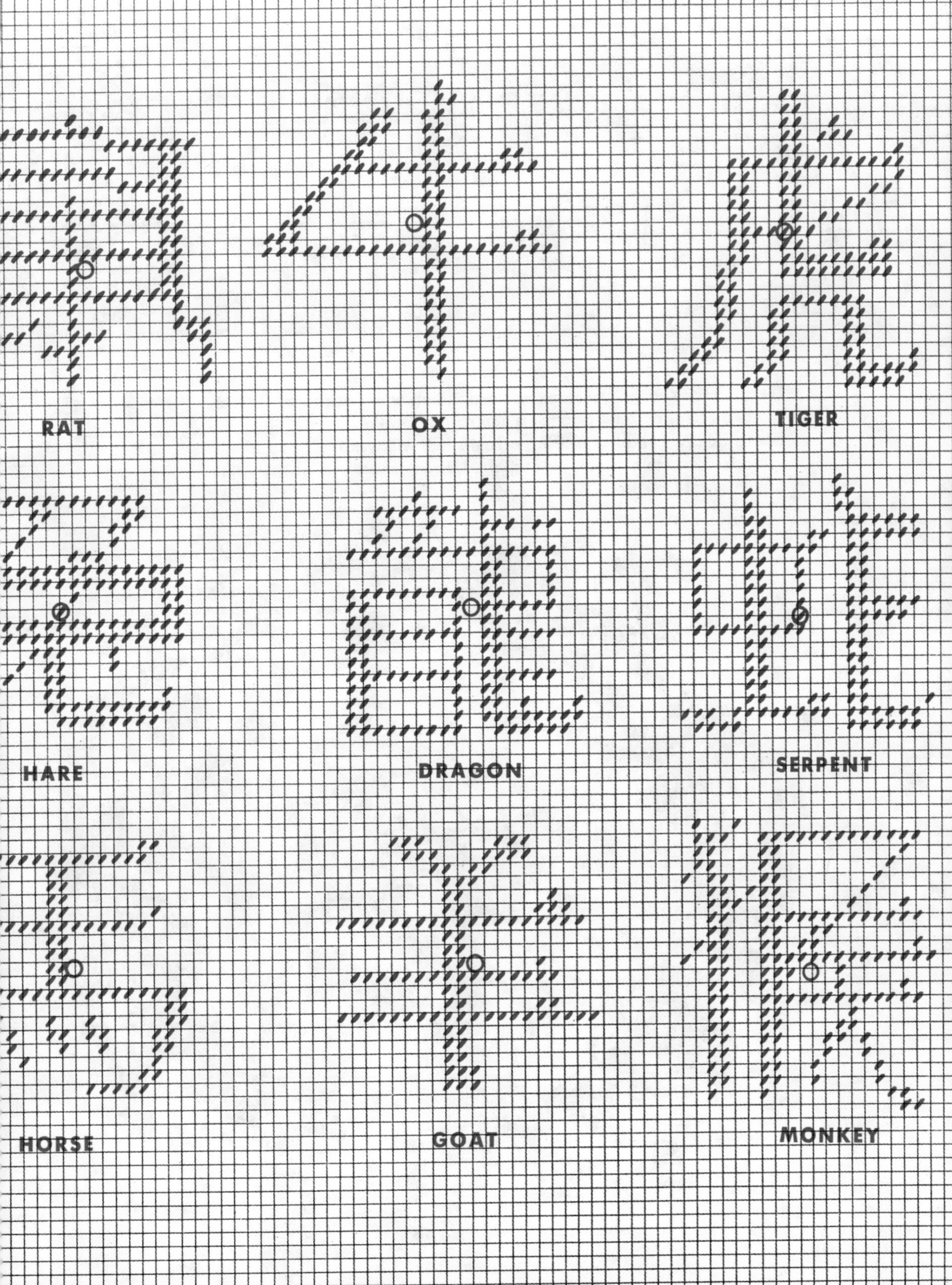
RAT
OX
TIGER
HARE
DRAGON
SERPENT
HORSE
GOAT
MONKEY

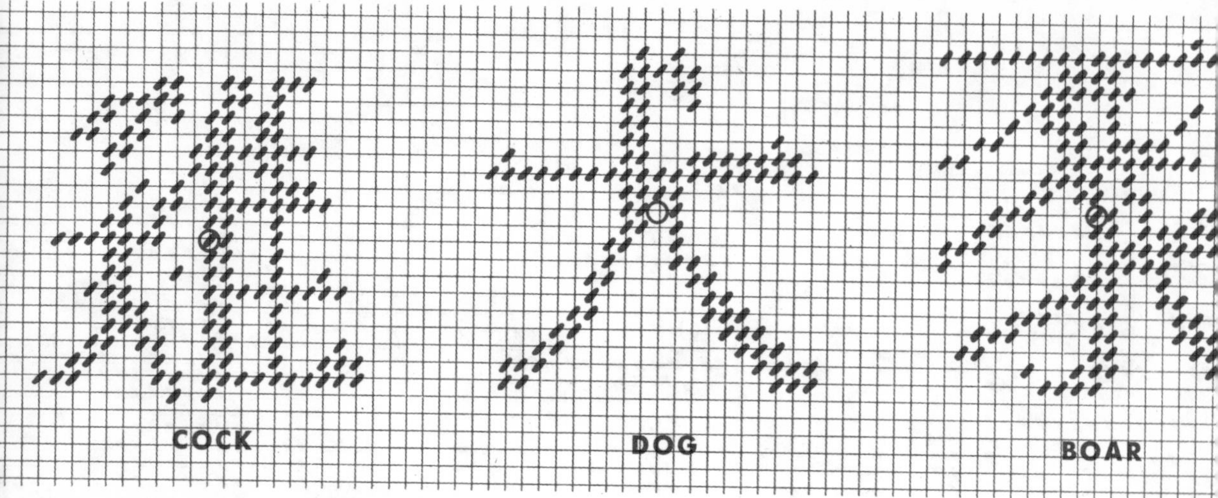


The Sign for Year of the Hare, corresponding with the zodiac Cancer, has been beaded here against a contrasting Basketweave background. Instead of making a Tent stitch with yarn, a bead is threaded on a thin needle and stitched down. The piece makes up into a tiny, ornate coaster.

**Double strand on 14-ct. canvas**
**height: 17 threads, average**

Several Hebrew words are included here in a style based on modern Hebraic writing. The words are written and read from right to left. No centers for the characters are indicated, since the characters are meant to be used in the words shown, aligned along a common base rather than individually.

The picture on page 104 shows "Hi" done in gold thread for a coaster.

L'HAIM (TO LIFE)

B'RUHIM

HABAIM

(WELCOME, BLESSED BE WHO ENTER)

SHALOM (PEACE)
MAZAL TOV (CONGRATULATIONS)
Leave space after third character
HI (LIFE)
SHADDAI (ALMIGHTY GOD)

Another coaster contains the Hebrew saying, "Hi," meaning Life. The characters are stitched in metallic thread, which makes them stand out from the Persian yarn background.

**Double strand on 14-ct. canvas**
**height: 16 threads**

The Greek letters can be used to show fraternity and sorority symbols and are useful in some ecclesiastical work.

Color pictures showing Greek letters appear on page iii and page viii.

ALPHA
BETA
GAMMA
DELTA
EPSILON
ZETA
ETA
THETA
IOTA
KAPPA
LAMBDA
MU

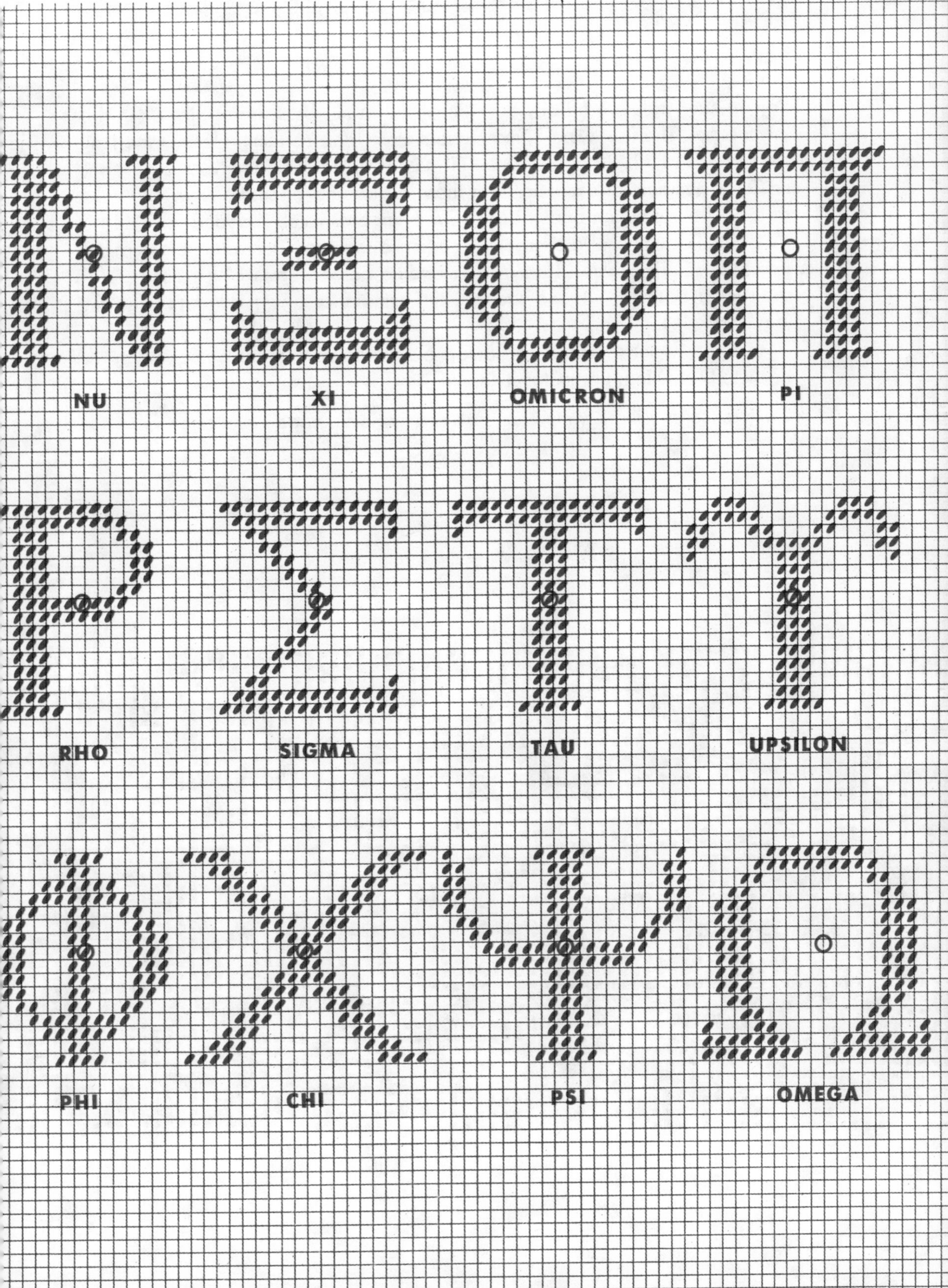
NU
XI
OMICRON
PI
RHO
SIGMA
TAU
UPSILON
PHI
CHI
PSI
OMEGA

# ROMAN NUMERALS

**Double strand on 14-ct. canvas**
**height: 7 threads**

Roman Numerals are an obvious alternative to numbers, especially when dating a piece. The following Roman letters were used as numerals until the tenth century A.D.: I=1, V=5, X=10, L=50, C=100, D=500, and M=1000.

Other numbers are formed from these by adding or subtracting. The value of a symbol following another of equal or greater value is added (e.g., III=3, XV=15). The value of a symbol preceding one of greater value is subtracted (e.g., IV=4). The value of a symbol standing between two of greater value is subtracted from that of the second, the remainder being added to the first (e.g., XIX=19).

You may want to make up Roman Numerals from other alphabets in this book to fit in with a particular style.

Color pictures using Roman Numerals are found on page ii and page viii.

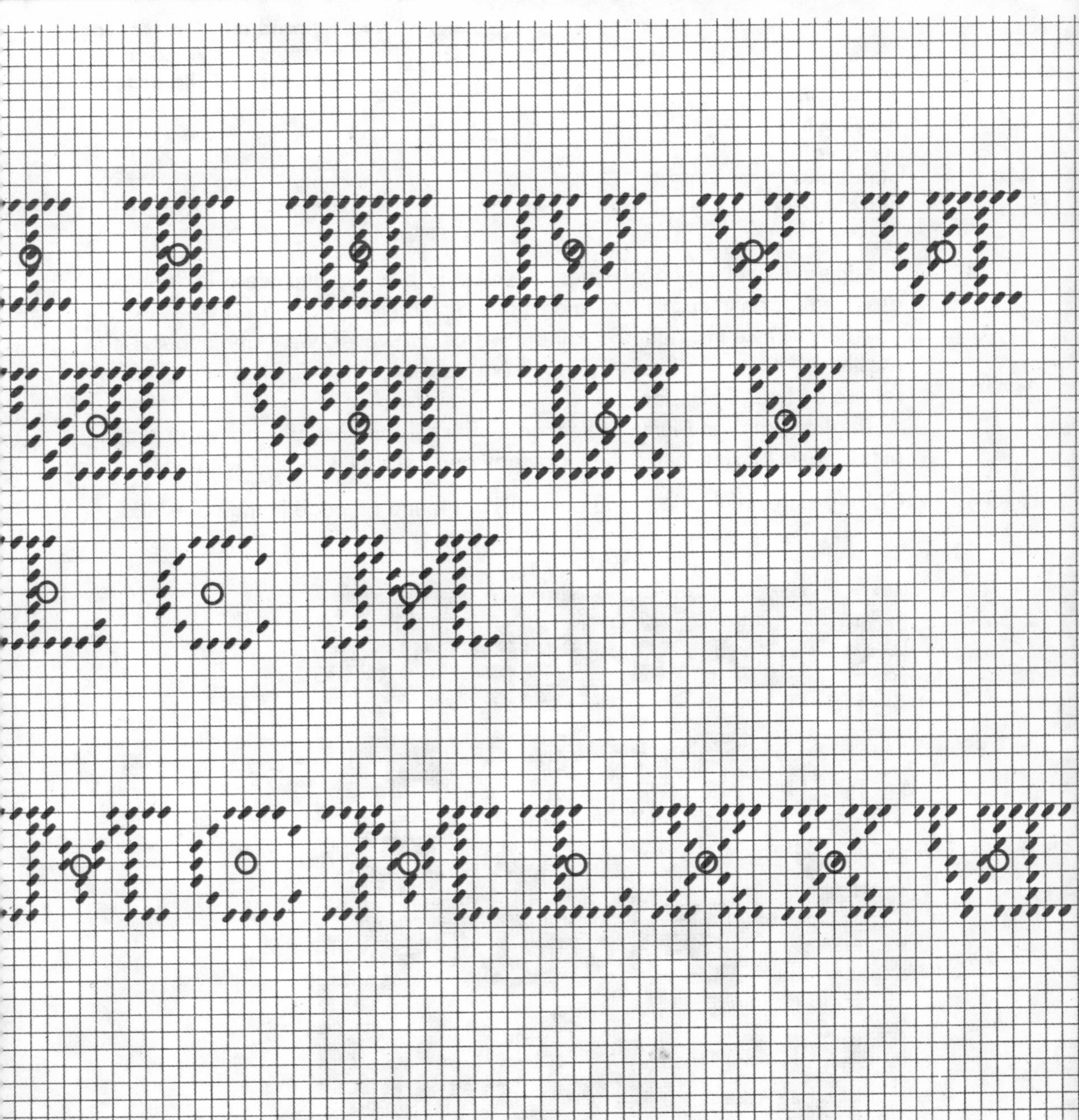

# INTERNATIONAL ALPHABET FLAGS

**Double strand on 14-ct. canvas**
**height: letters – 11 threads**
**numbers – 12 threads**

***Color code***
**gray=white**
**red=red**
**pink=blue**
**black=yellow**
**black o=black**

The International Alphabet Flags are used in boating and were undoubtedly designed for an intense visual impact. Usually the letters are grouped vertically on hoists from left to right to spell out words. However, we "landlubbers" can use them with poetic license to spell out names or words. They are excellent for use on belts, for instance.

The International Numeral Pennants offer still another alternative to writing out numbers for dates, and they look gay and colorful with the alphabet flags.

Color pictures of the flags and pennants are found on page ii and page vii.

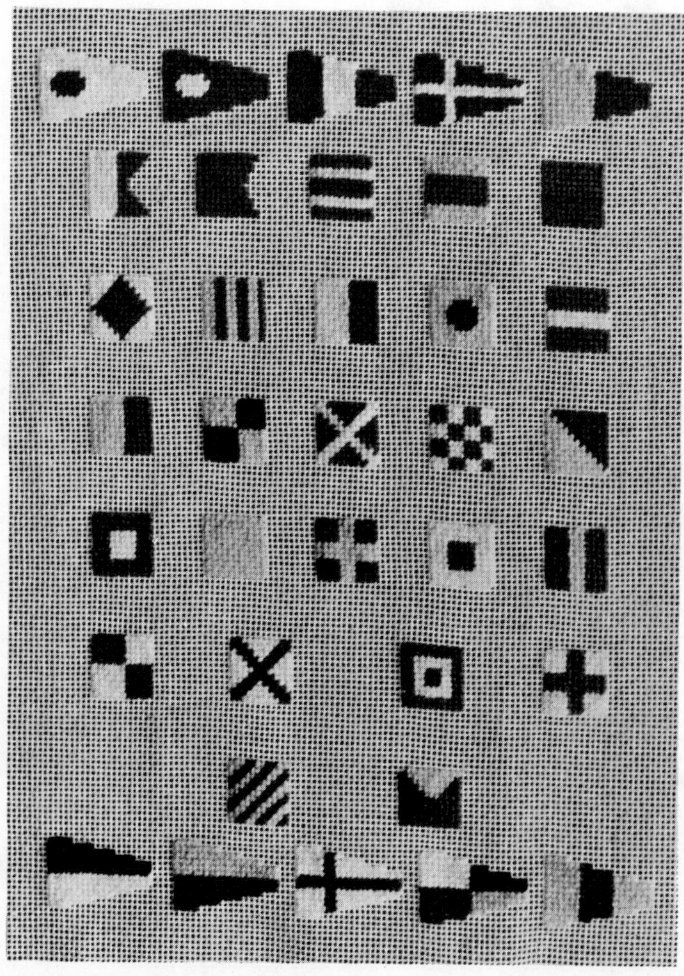

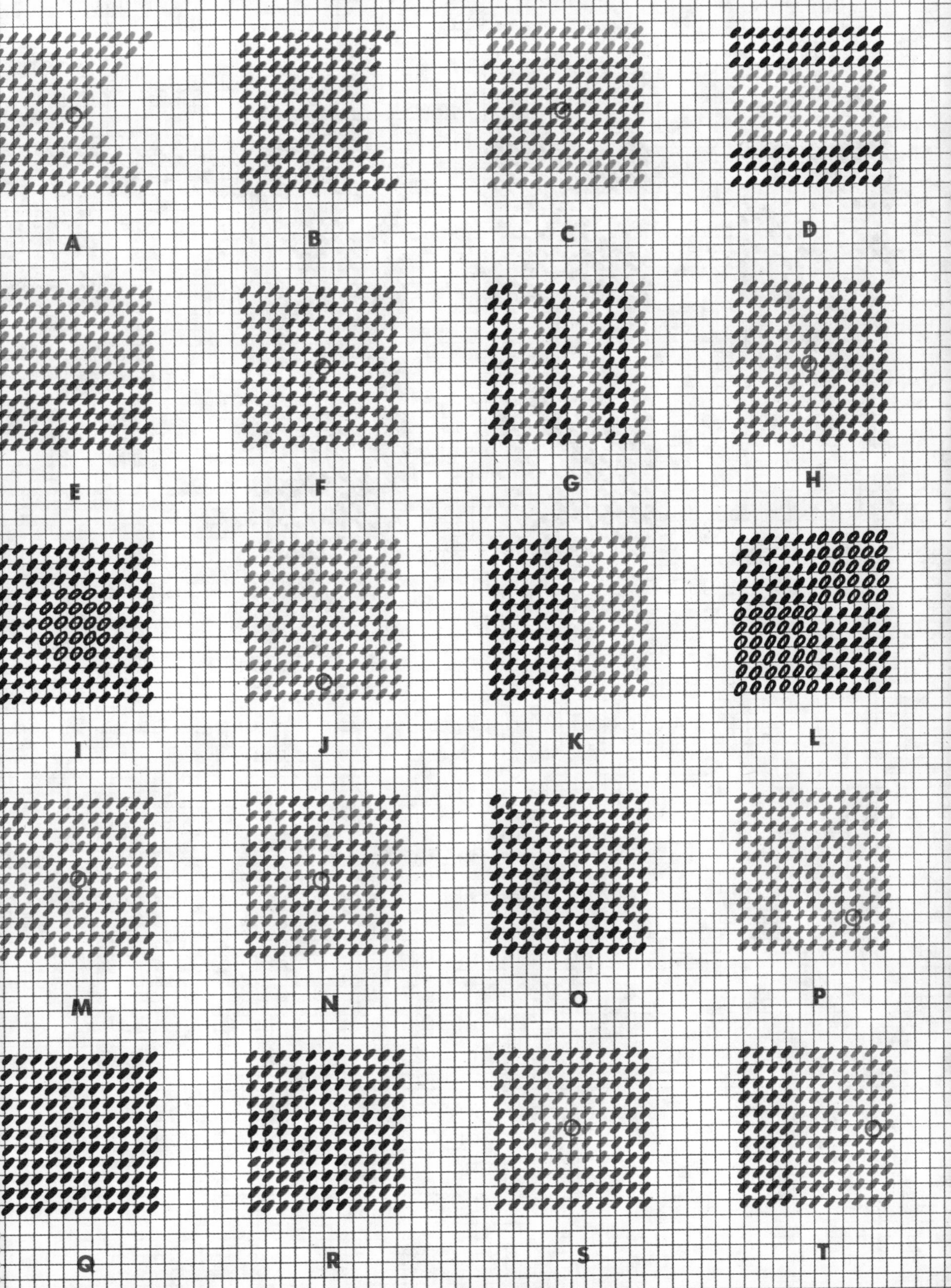
A
B
C
D
E
F
G
H
I
J
K
L
M
N
O
P
Q
R
S
T

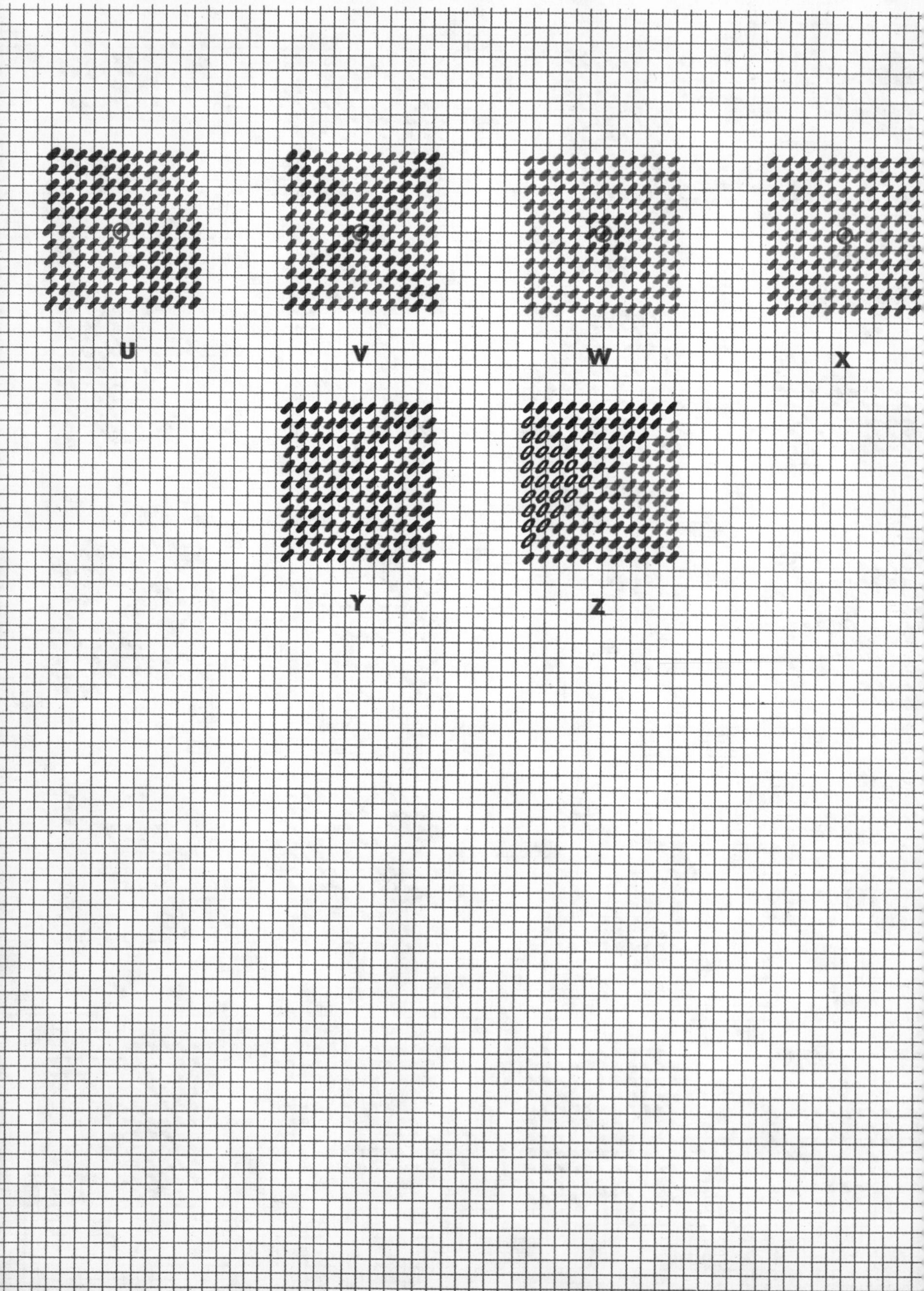
U
V
W
X
Y
Z

Roman Magesty letters are the central motifs for these needlepoint pieces. The "K" incorporates French Knots instead of Tent stitch in the flowers. The "N" insert has been blocked and stitched to a premade pillow, which is a relatively inexpensive project. The "V" is surrounded by a huge border in a bold four-way, or kaleidoscopic, Bargello pattern.

More purses! Four-way Bargello is used as a border around the Broadway Stars monogram. The Roman Magesty "S" is attractively stitched on the flap of a premounted Naugahyde shoulder bag, and the Roman Magesty "A" personalizes a handsome tote worked in mock plaid. The Bermuda bag, in an interlaced ribbon pattern, has a Contemporary Stripe monogram in bold colors.

Old Western letters are used to write out the motto on the interlaced ribbon racquet cover. The hat, premounted, sports a needlepointed visor in Script. The needlepoint plaid racquet cover has a Gothic alphabet motto. P.S. Men love tennis racquet covers, too.

This elegant evening bag is worked on needlepoint canvas. Instead of stitching with yarn, a bead is threaded on a thin needle and worked like a Tent stitch to fasten it down. The Roman Magesty "O" is interesting and large enough to make up the whole design.

A fancy monogram decorates the cover of this velvet jewelry box. The needlepoint piece is edged with cording and sewn to velvet. Appropriately, the initials are worked in large and small Monogram Blocks.

This needlepoint picture represents the logo of a T.V. talk show. The letters were enlarged by projecting a slide on the wall and tracing around the image. A four-way Bargello border adds interest to the design.

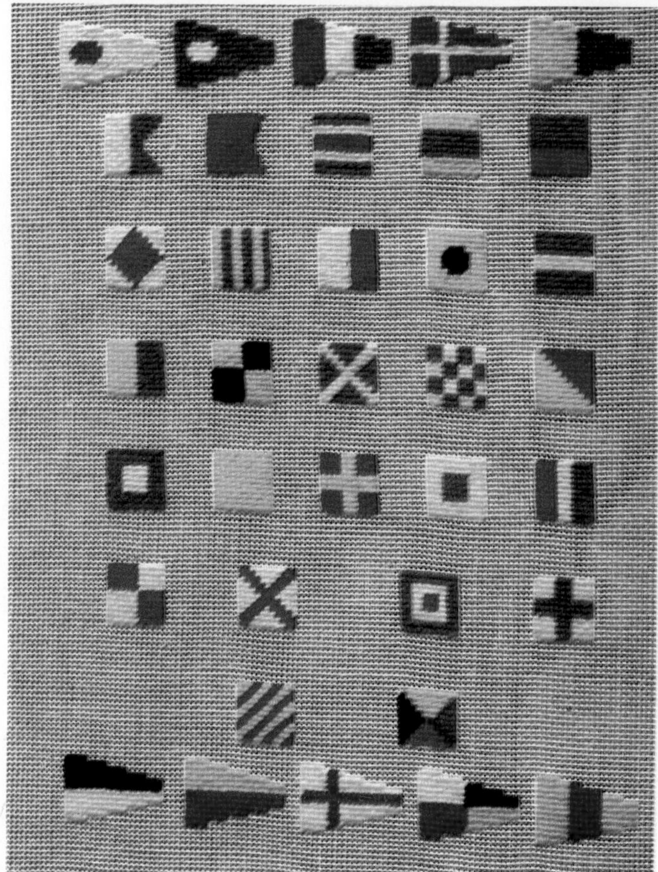

The International Alphabet Flags and Numeral Pennants are bright and attractive enough to stand on their own as a design and are shown here for your "viewing pleasure."

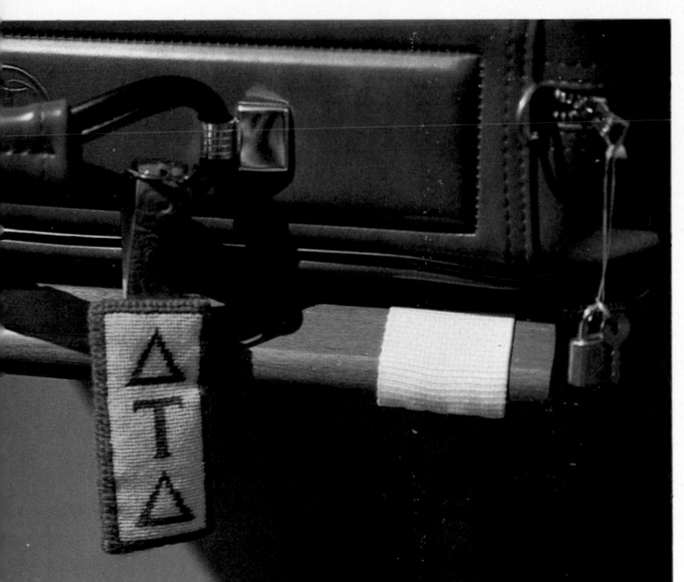


A luggage tag is worked here in a Greek fraternity symbol. The reverse side is also stitched, with the initials of the recipient of this unique needlepoint gift.

Name blocks make marvelous gifts. The ones shown here are in Script and Classic. The scrapbook insert is worked in crossword puzzle fashion, using Chinese Cross, a variation of Contemporary Stripe, and Slim Line. The address book has a needlepoint insert with Smyrna letters. The "Now I lay me down to sleep" phrase is worked in Typewriter Print; the piece will be mounted as a typewriter cover.

This magnificent butler's tray displays the initials of husband and wife and their three children in an interlaced band pattern using several stitches and needlepoint plaid. Early Sampler, Carnival, and Roman Numerals are combined with striking Turkey Tufted letters.

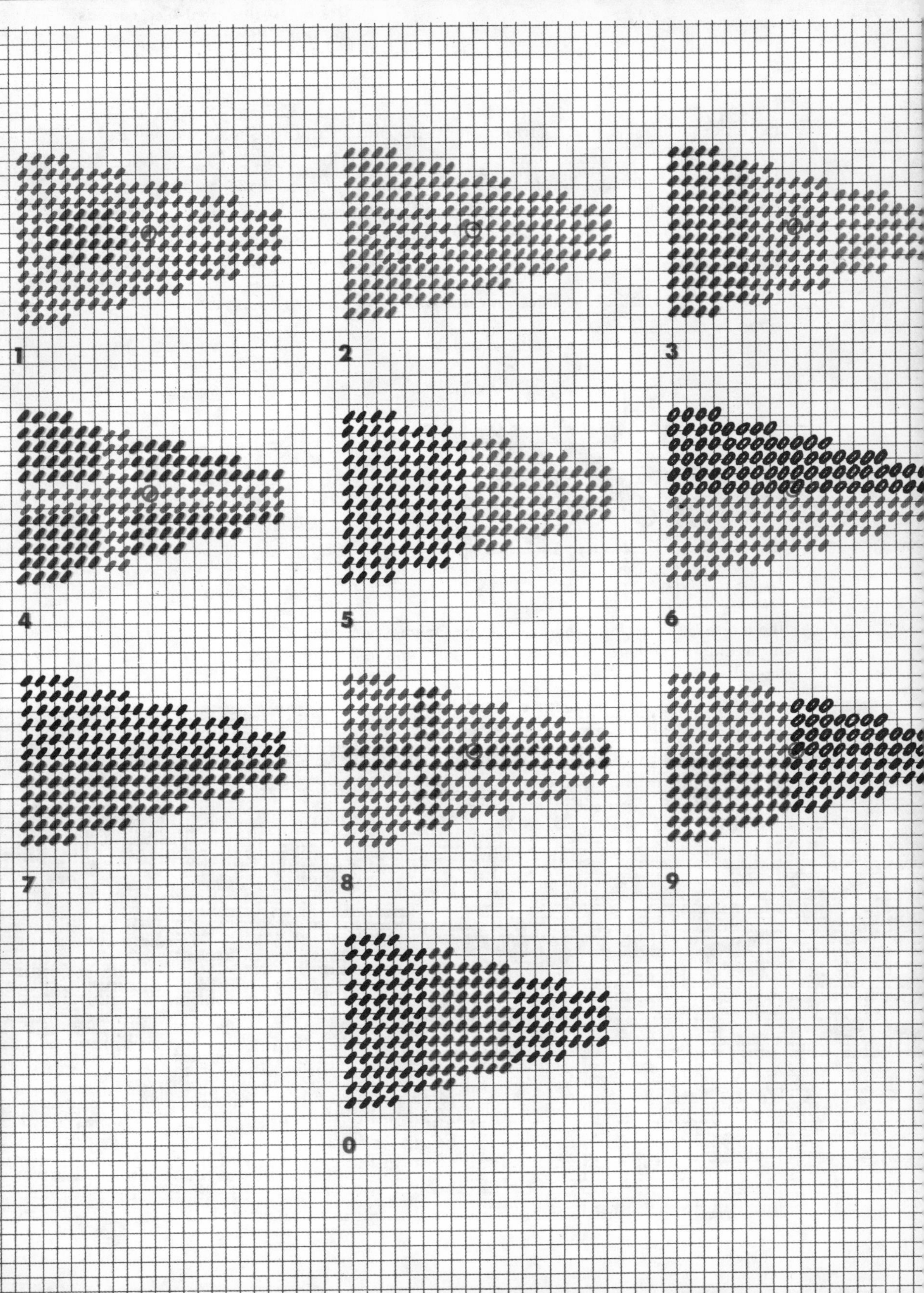

1
2
3
4
5
6
7
8
9
0

# INTERNATIONAL MORSE CODE

**Double strand on 14-ct. canvas**
**height: 2 threads**

Put hidden meaning in a border composed of dots and dashes that spell out a name or sentence. Use as a guide the diagram of the Mosaic stitch on page 63 for the dots, and the diagram of the Oblique stitch (below) for the dashes. Each dot should be 2 threads wide and 2 threads tall. Each dash is 6 threads wide and 2 threads tall. There are 6 threads between letters and 10 threads between words.

Color pictures using the International Morse Code are found on page ii and page iii.

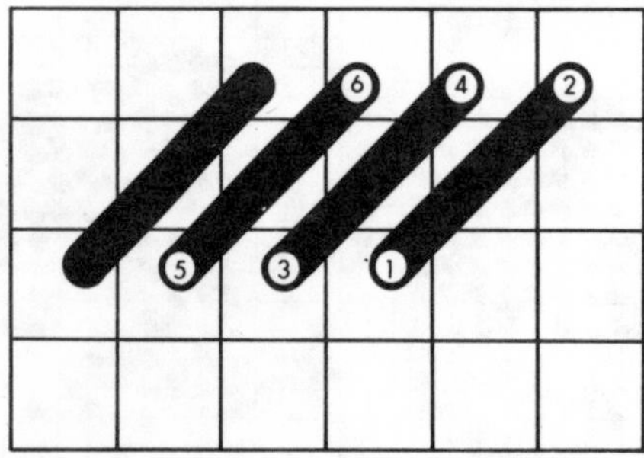


**The Morse Code dashes are based on the Oblique or Slanted Gobelin stitch, diagramed here. Each stitch slants up 2 and to the right 2 canvas threads.**

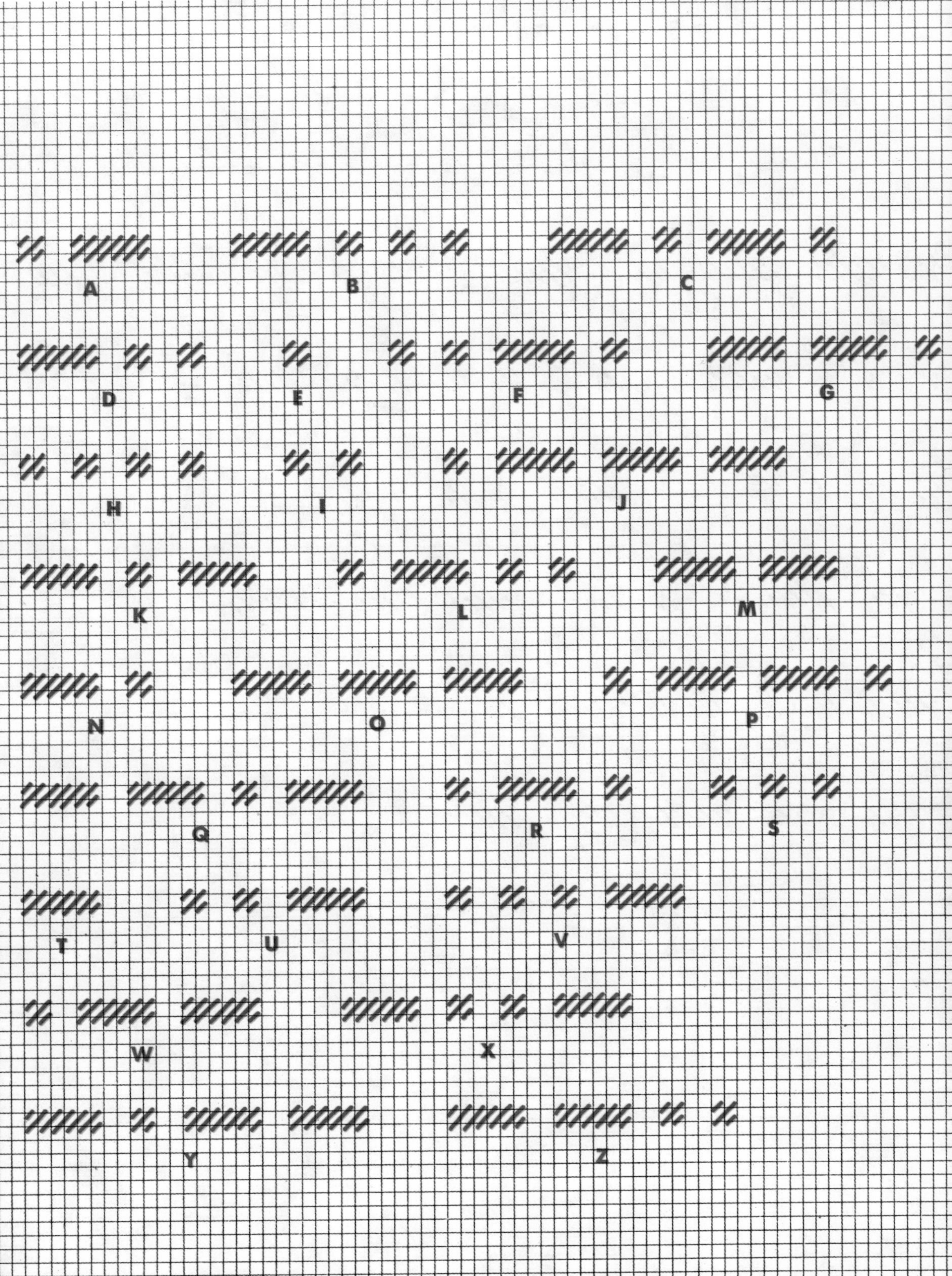
A
B
C
D
E
F
G
H
I
J
K
L
M
N
O
P
Q
R
S
T
U
V
W
X
Y
Z

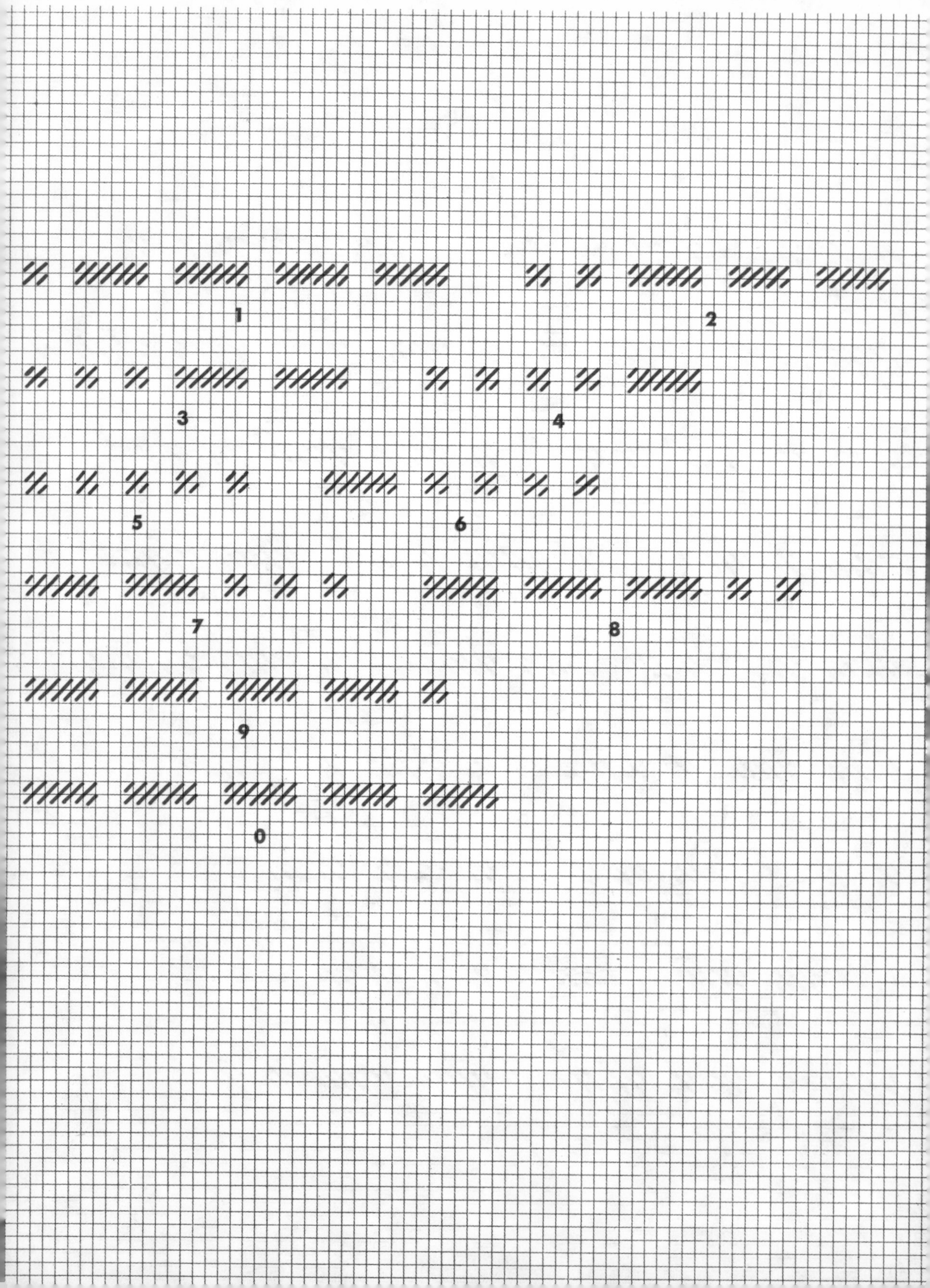

1

2

3

4

5

6

7

8

9

0

Morse Code and International Signal Flags are combined with Roman Magesty "T" for a needlepoint ice bucket insert, also shown in color on page ii. The piece is shown before mounting to give a better idea of how the design was laid out. Once the letter was worked, all counting and spacing was done to right and left using the "T" border as a guide. Note that the vines have been "borrowed" from the center and used as decoration at the sides. Make sure when turning a motif sideways that your stitches all go in the same direction or you will have difficulty stitching in the background.

# ROMAN MAGESTY ALPHABET

**Double strand on 14-ct. canvas**
**block size – height: 70 threads**
**width: 65 threads**

The alphabet presented on the following pages provides the stitcher with multiple opportunities to embellish needlepoint with initials or to use these letters as central design motifs. The letters have been worked in identically counted blocks so that the designs can be interchanged.

The A, S, V, X, Y, and Z are decorated with formal geometric borders. B, C, G, I, J, K, M, N, O, and P are adorned with ornate floral motifs. D, E, F, H, L, Q, R, U, and W are based on lace patterns and small repeat patterns. The T, obviously a favorite with the authors, is a fanciful design that can be transposed onto several of the letters with vertical straight lines. Sources for the designs span many kinds and styles of embroidery.

The versatility of the alphabet does not end with "swapping" designs from one letter to another. The letters are large enough to work in stitches other than Tent, and various canvas stitches can be introduced into the patterns, as demonstrated in the finished samples presented on the following pages.

The letters are positioned in a rectangle that is 70 threads high and 65 threads wide. Therefore, if you use 10-ct. canvas, each sample would be 7 inches high. A sample worked on 14-ct. canvas would be proportionately smaller.

Again, it is recommended that right-handed stitchers count from the center, working to the left and down on the outline of the letter and then filling in with Basketweave. Left-handed stitchers should start work to the right and up.

When transposing letters and designs, you may want to use gridded tracing paper to amalgamate a new letter-design combination before starting to stitch. The circles in this alphabet indicate the true center of each 70- by 65-thread block.

Beading follows the same grids and graphing that needlepoint does, and beads can easily be substituted for yarn. The Roman Magesty "O" and background are entirely beaded here. The purse is shown in color on page vi.

The "A" is worked in Tent with Mosaic around, and then the Greek Key design, again in Tent. This letter is used in a project that appears in color on page v.

Hungarian stitch has been used to make up the letter—Hungarian Ground is used in the background. The vine is worked on top of the other needlepoint in Chain stitch (page 154). A color picture of this letter is found on page iv.

Mosaic stitch is used to fill in the "C" and French Knots have added texture to the flower centers. This letter was blocked and mounted on a scrapbook cover.

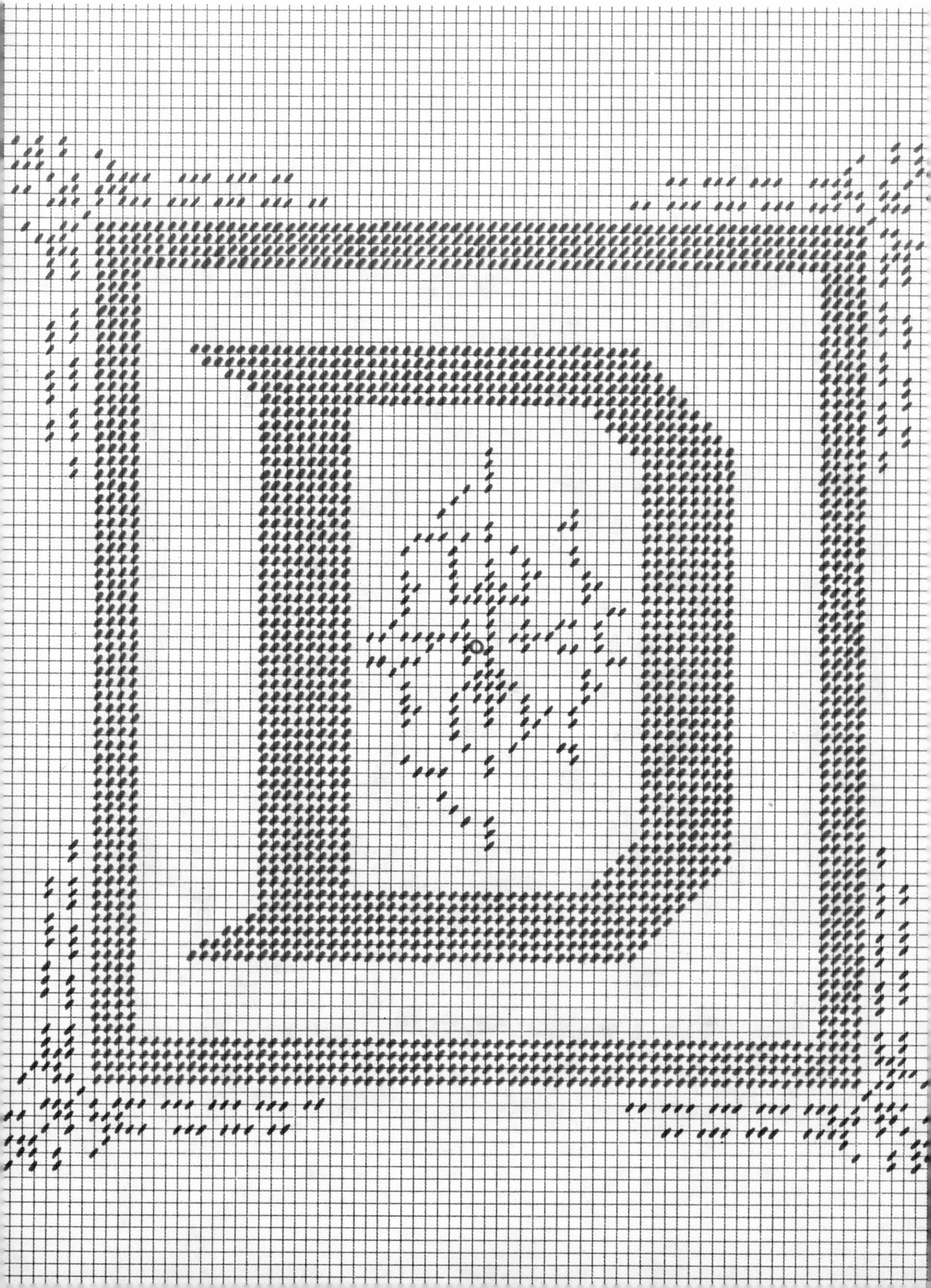

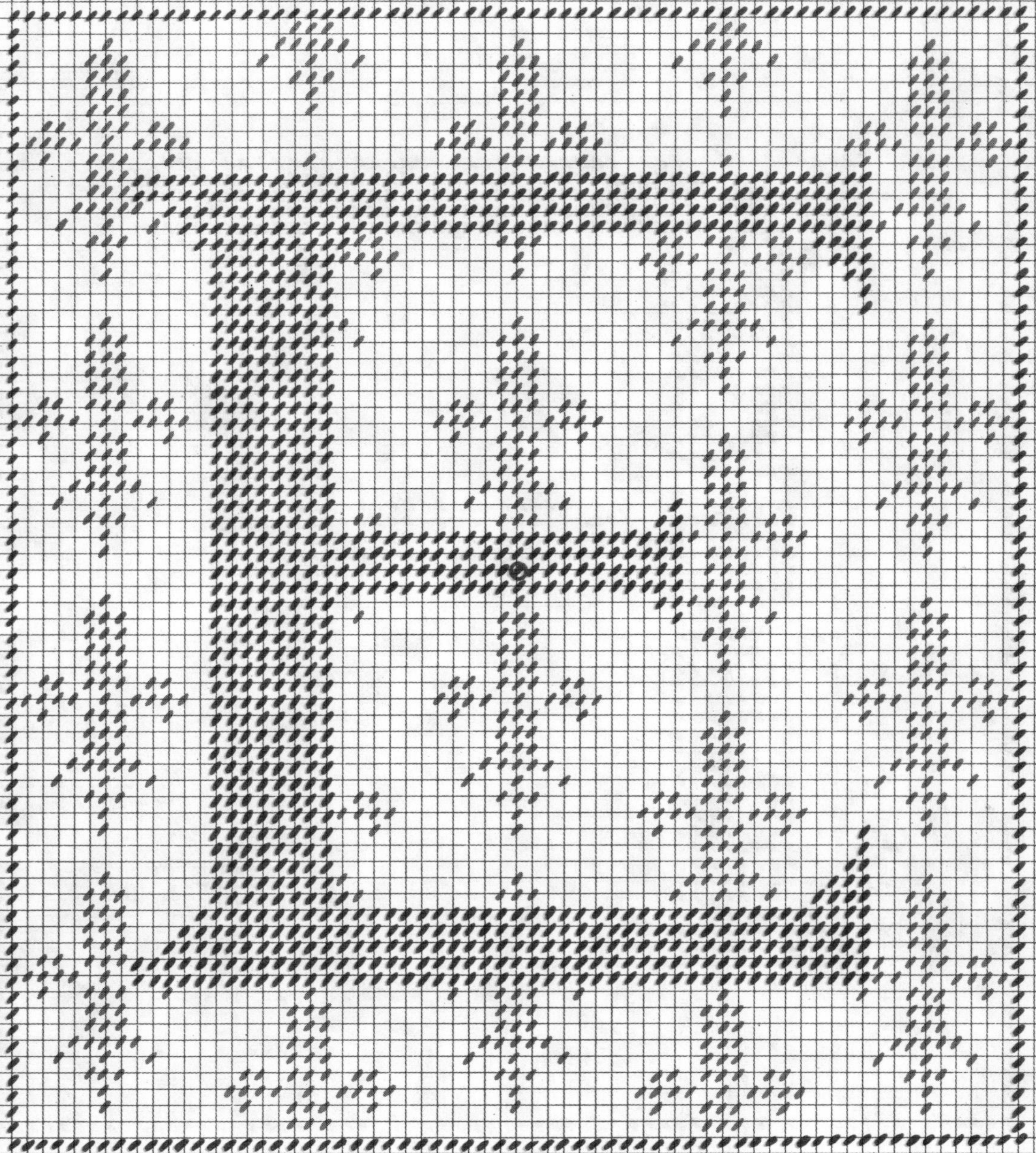

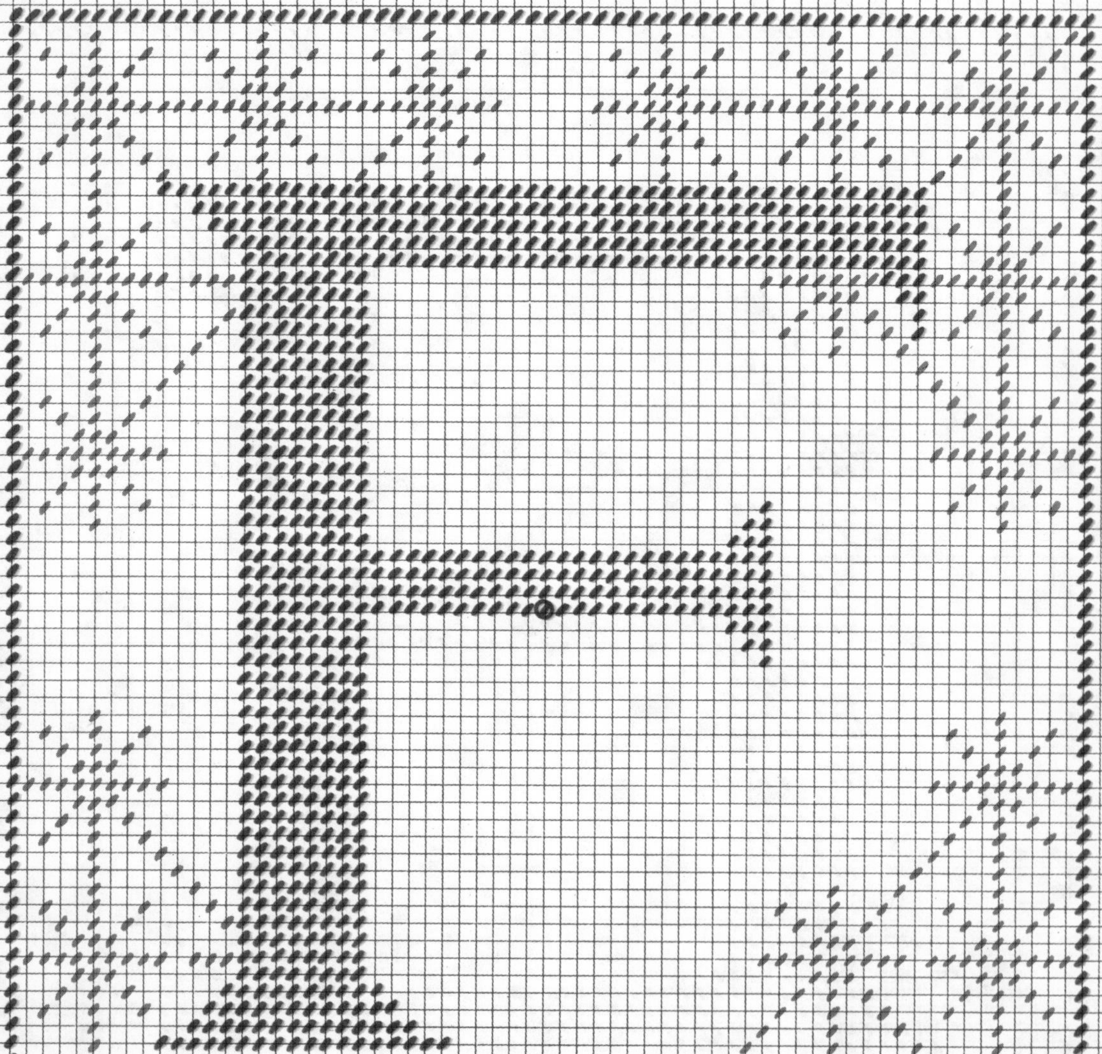

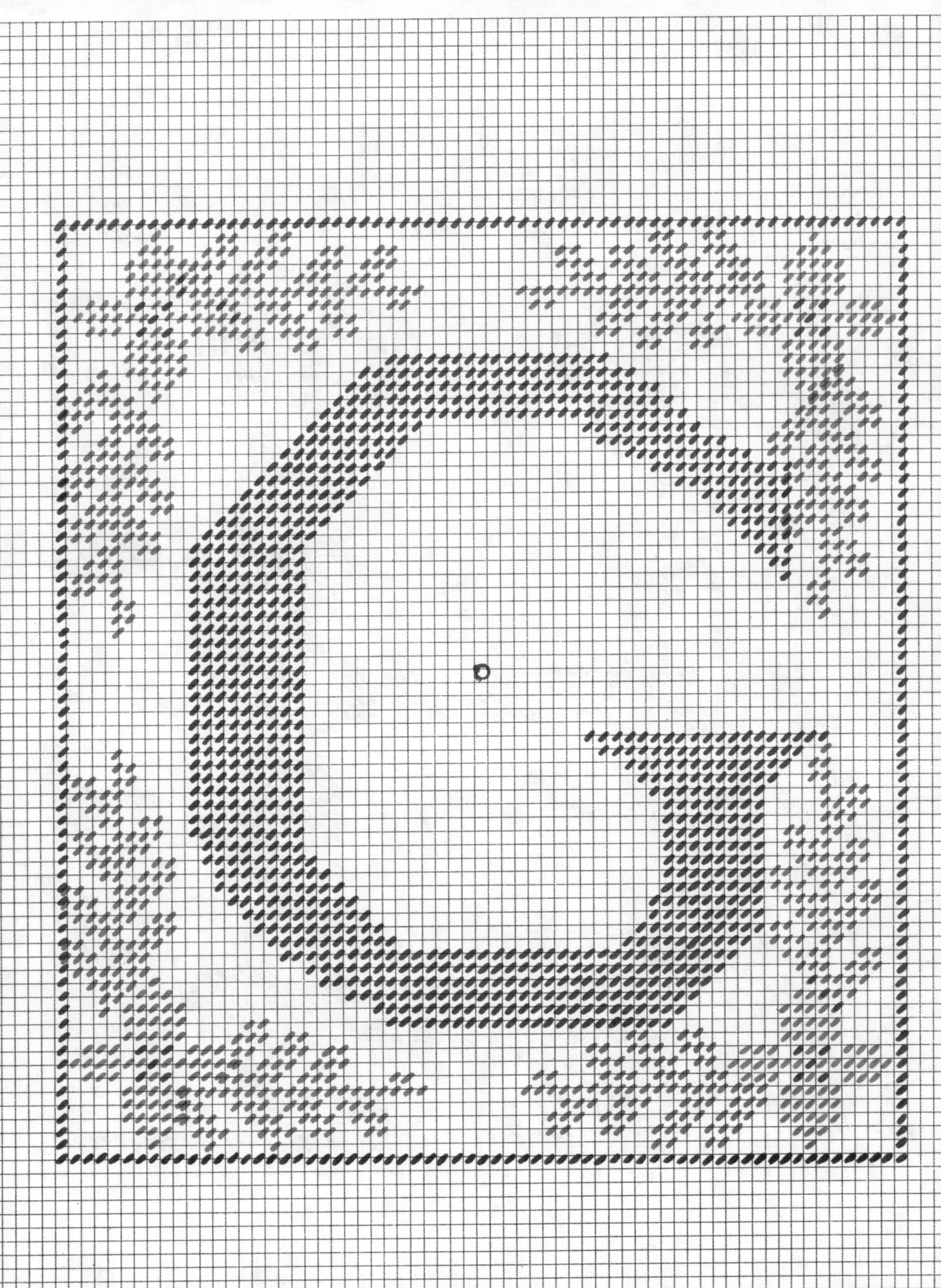

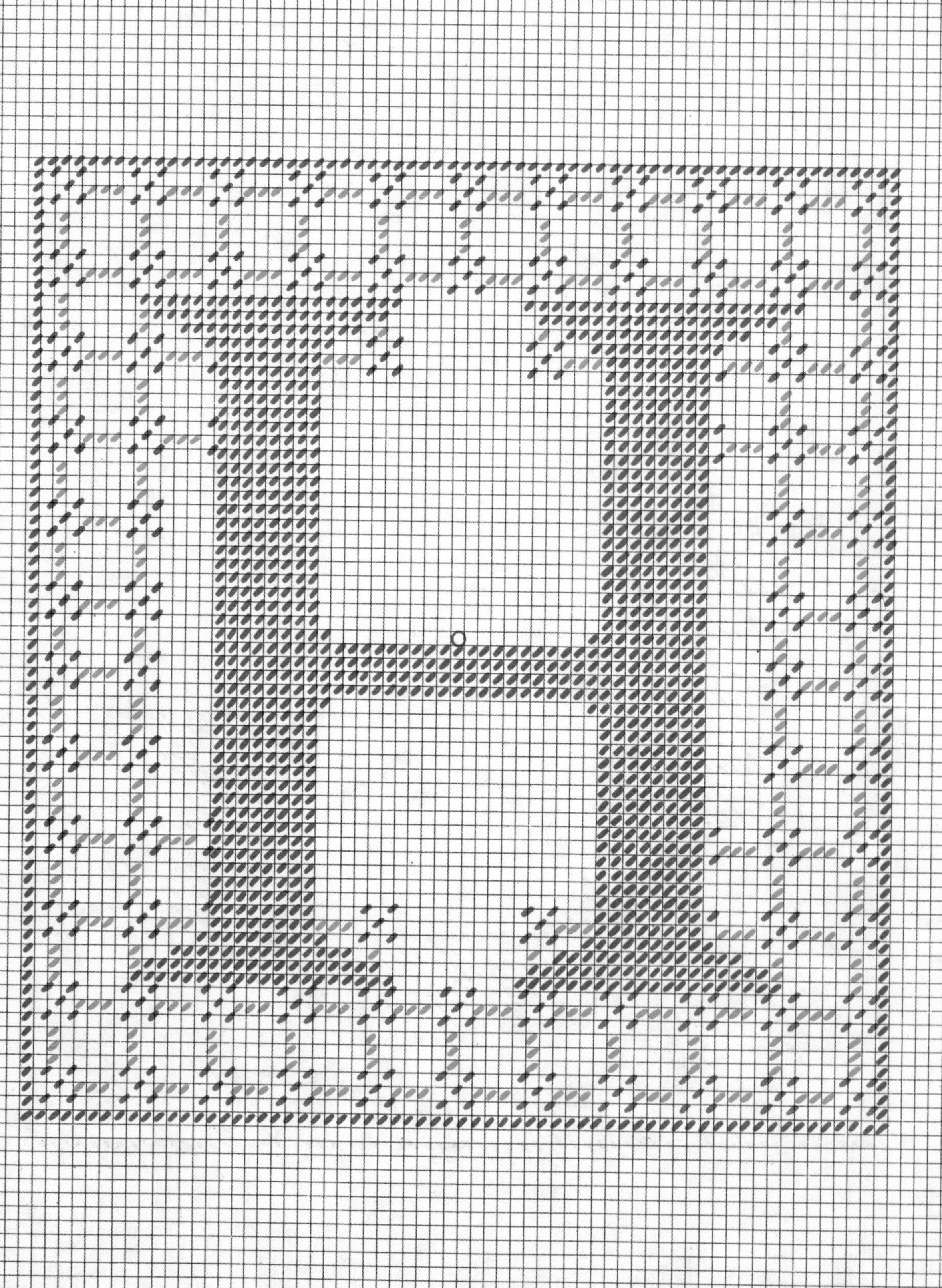

Several stitches have been incorporated in the "H," which is the central motif for a small lucite tray.

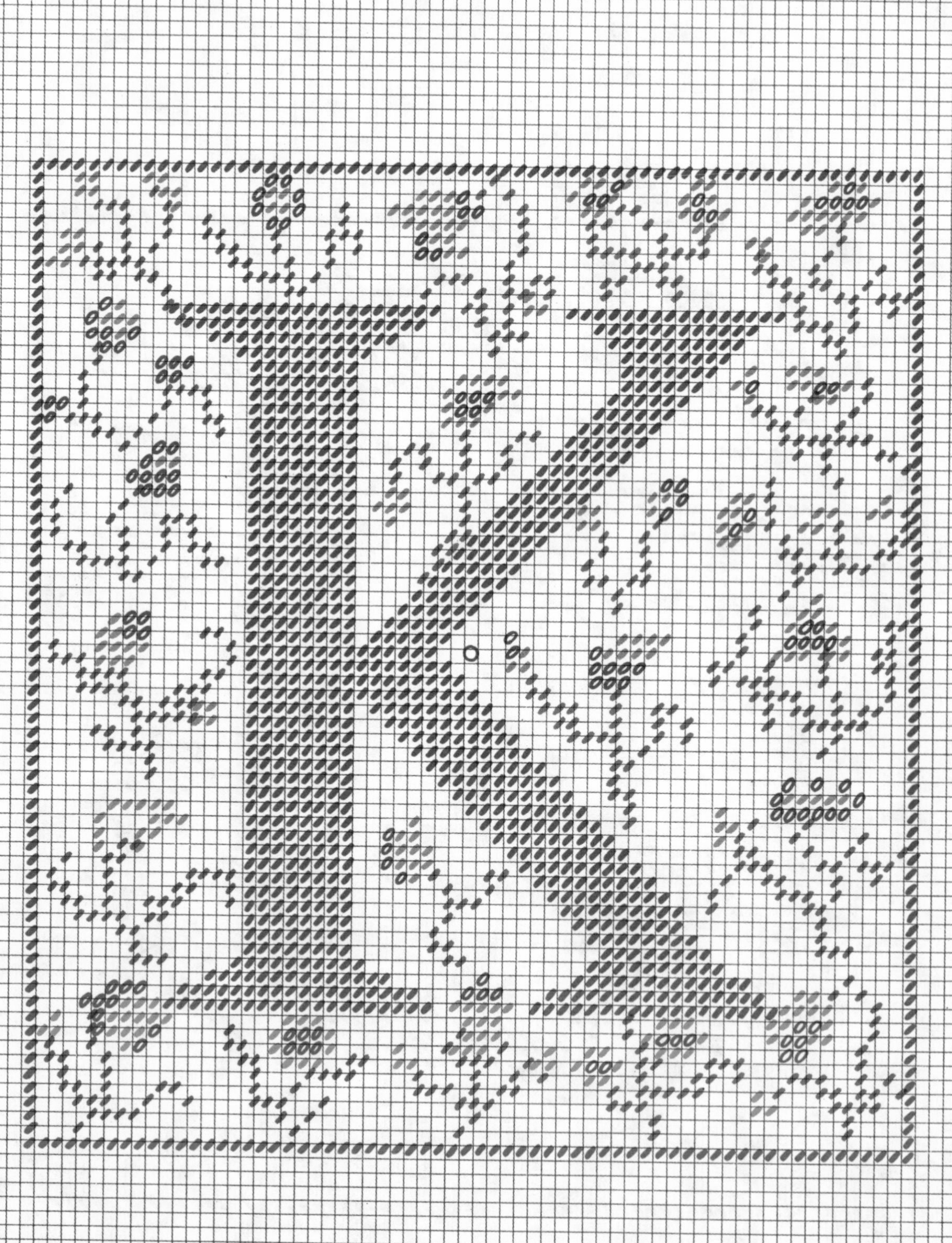

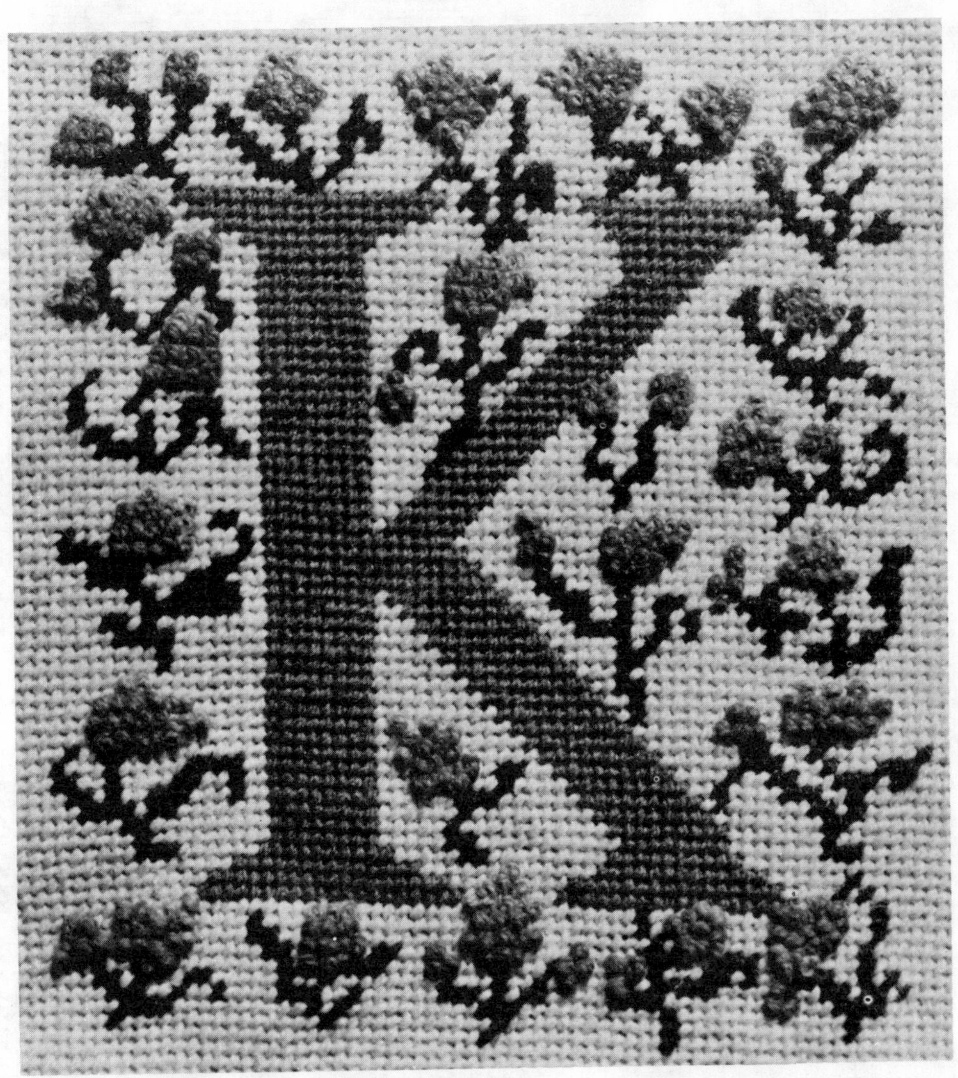

French Knots are used instead of Tent stitches for the flowers surrounding this "K." Also, the stitcher elected to leave out the border. The "K" is shown in color on page v.

This "N" has been worked in Tent stitch with a Flat stitch (page 72) variation for the background. The letter is shown in color on page v.

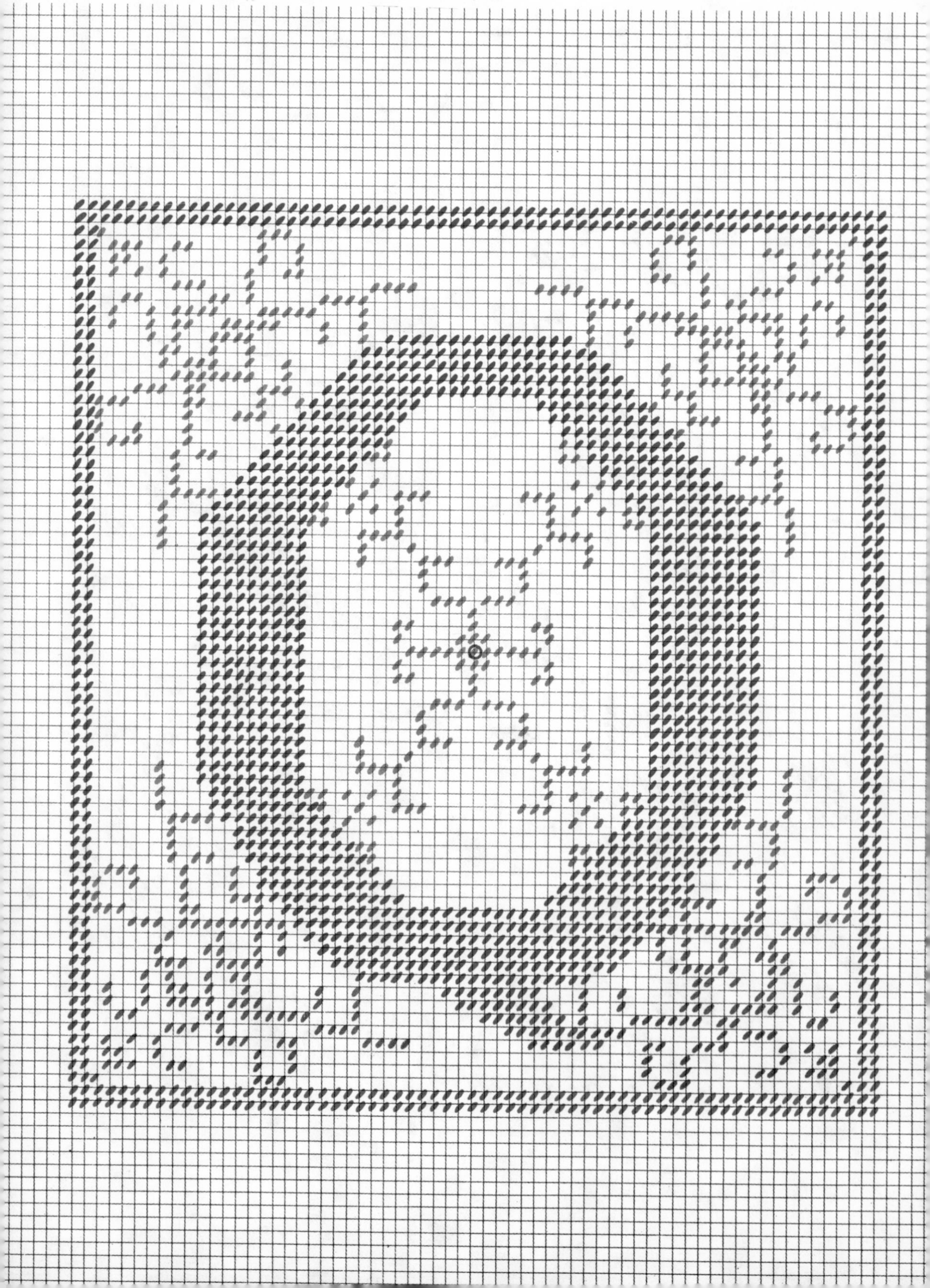

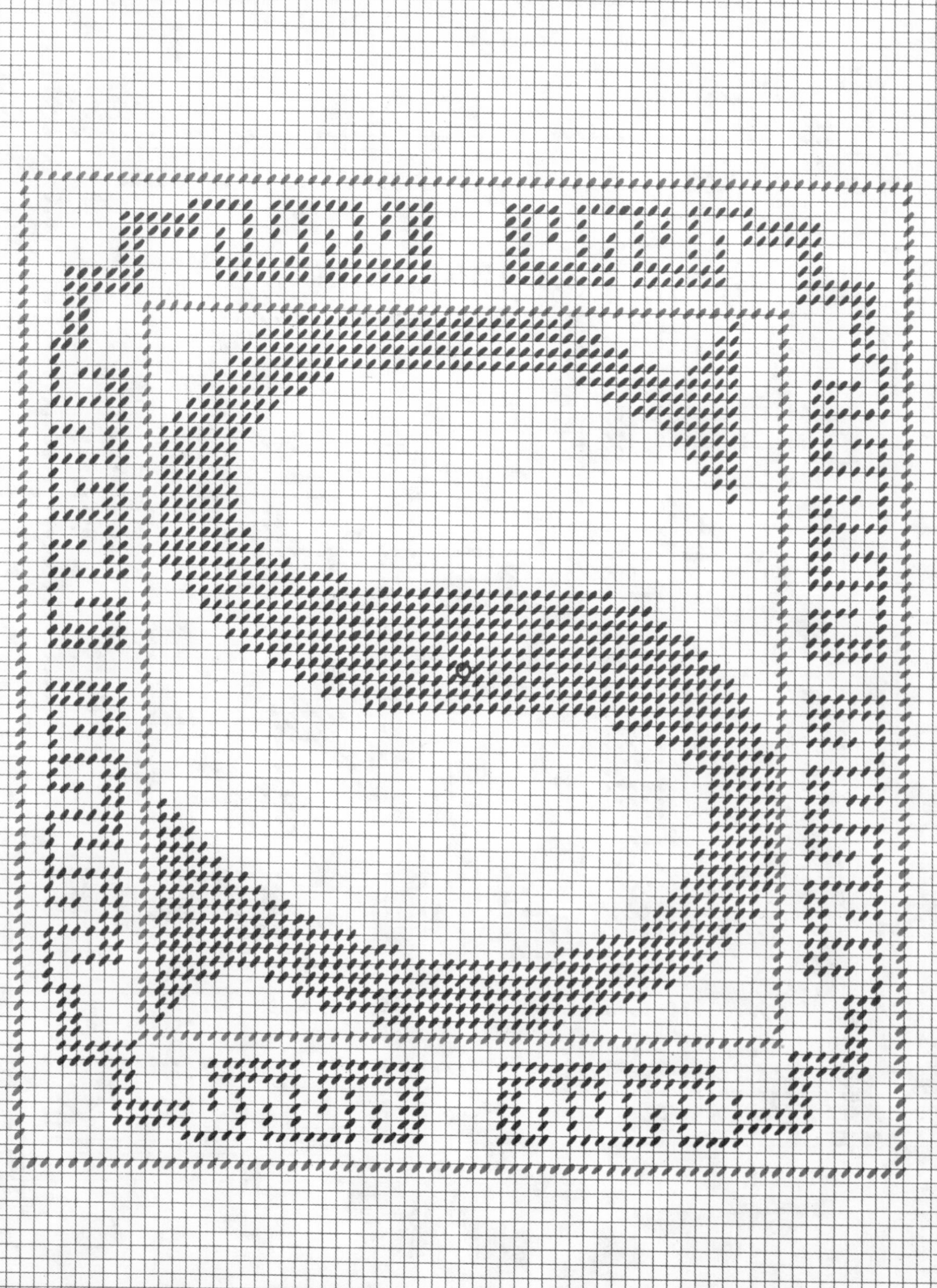

The Roman Magesty "S" is surrounded by Cashmere, a stitch pattern quite like Mosaic and Flat. The letter is shown in color on page v.

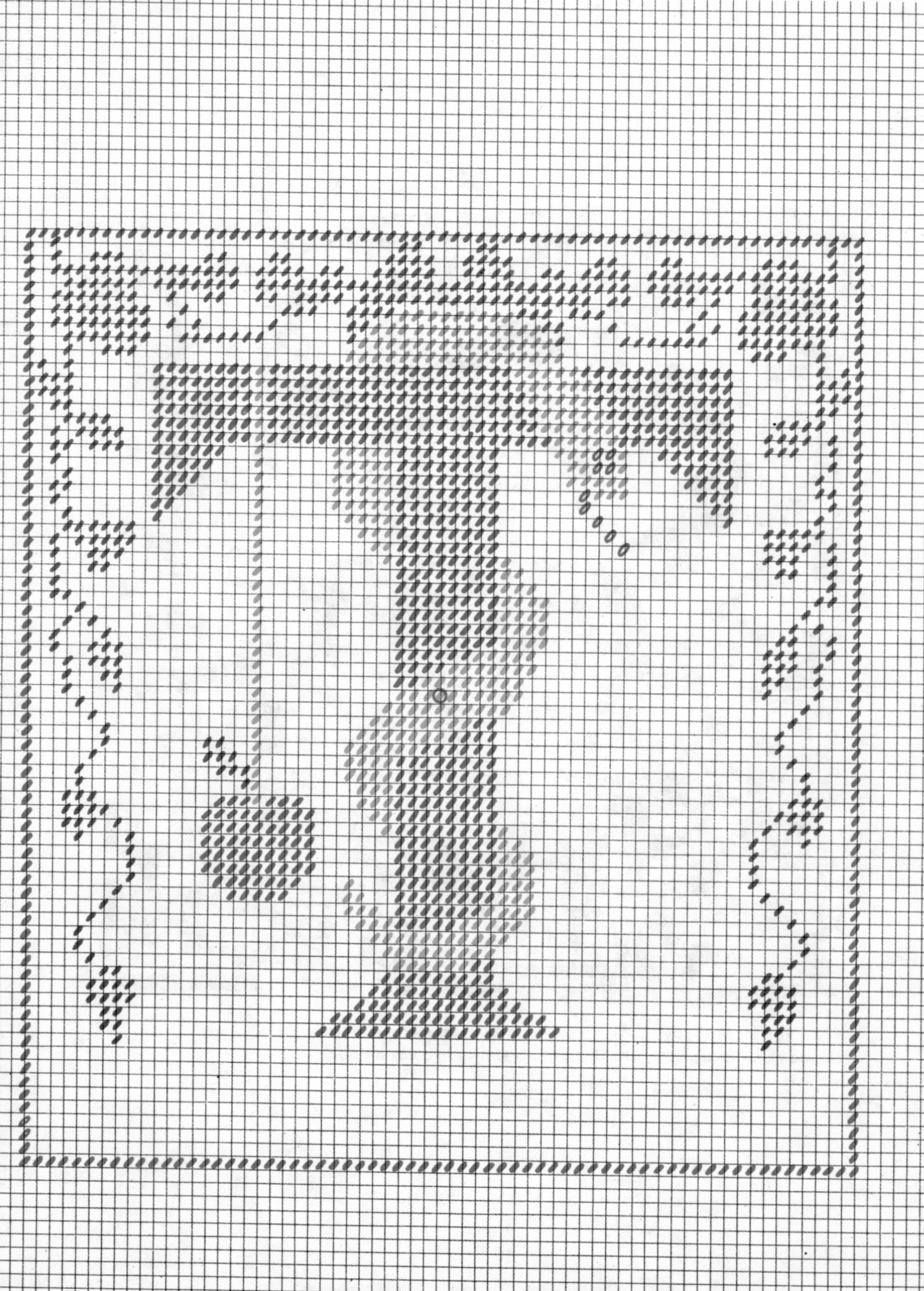

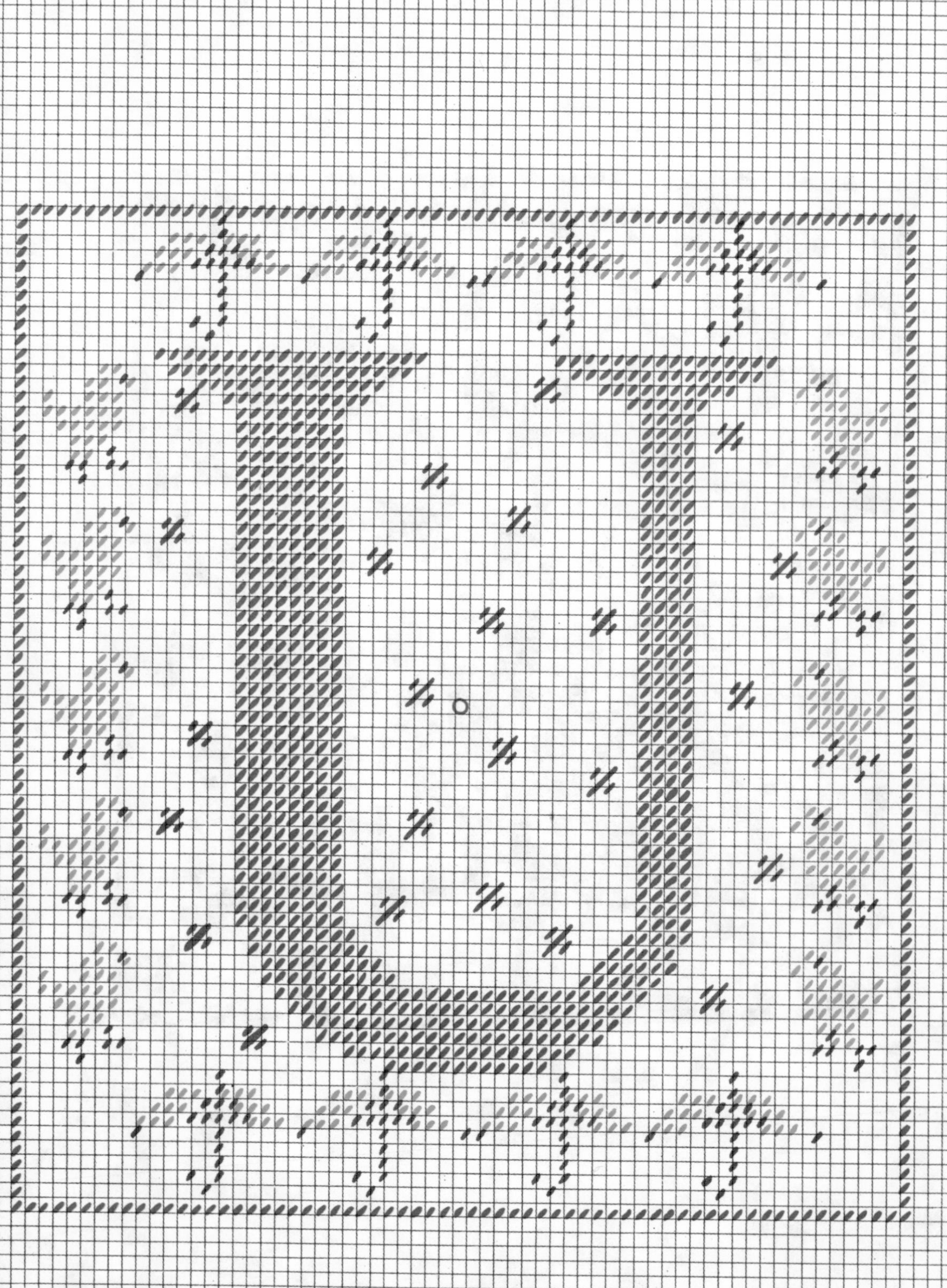

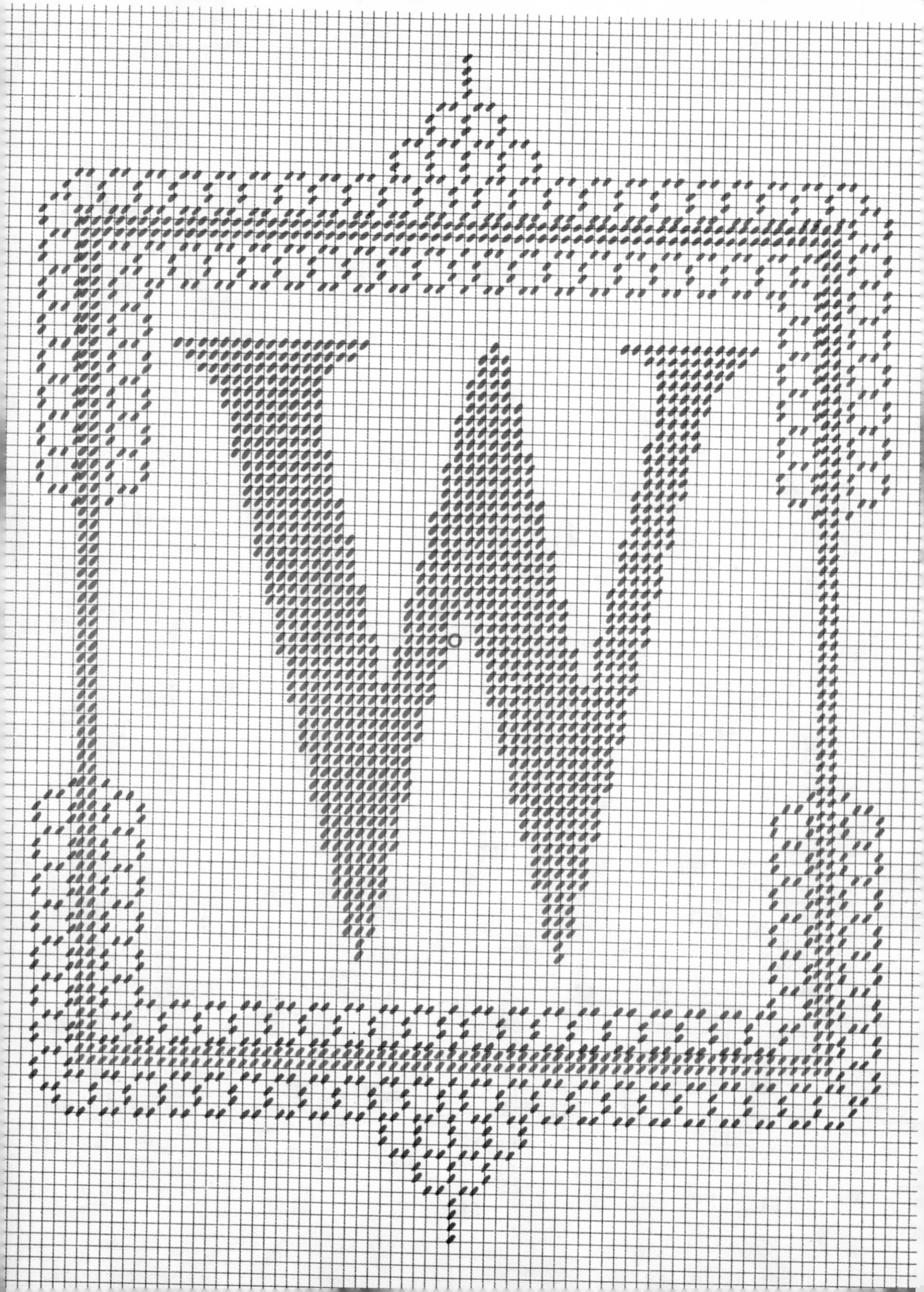

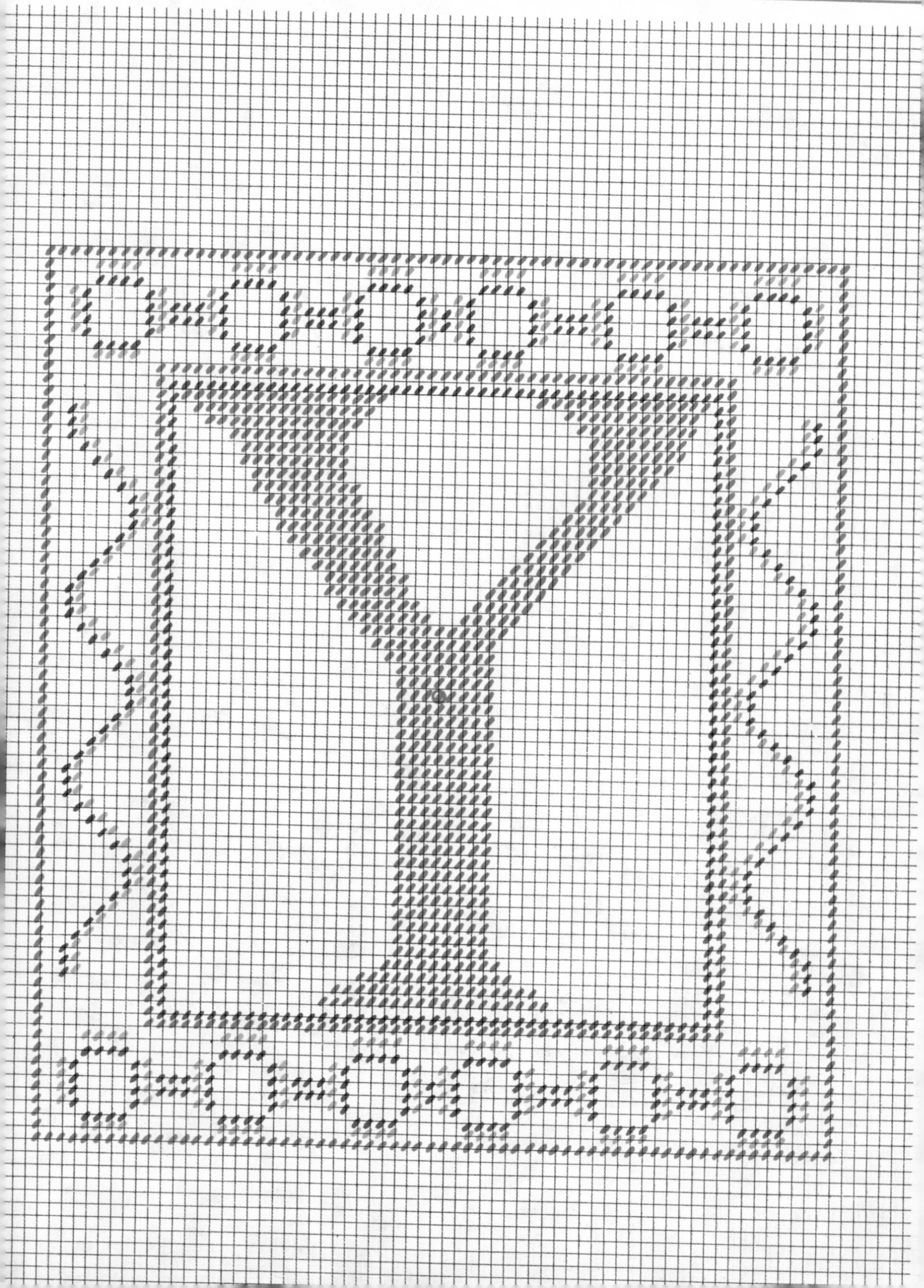

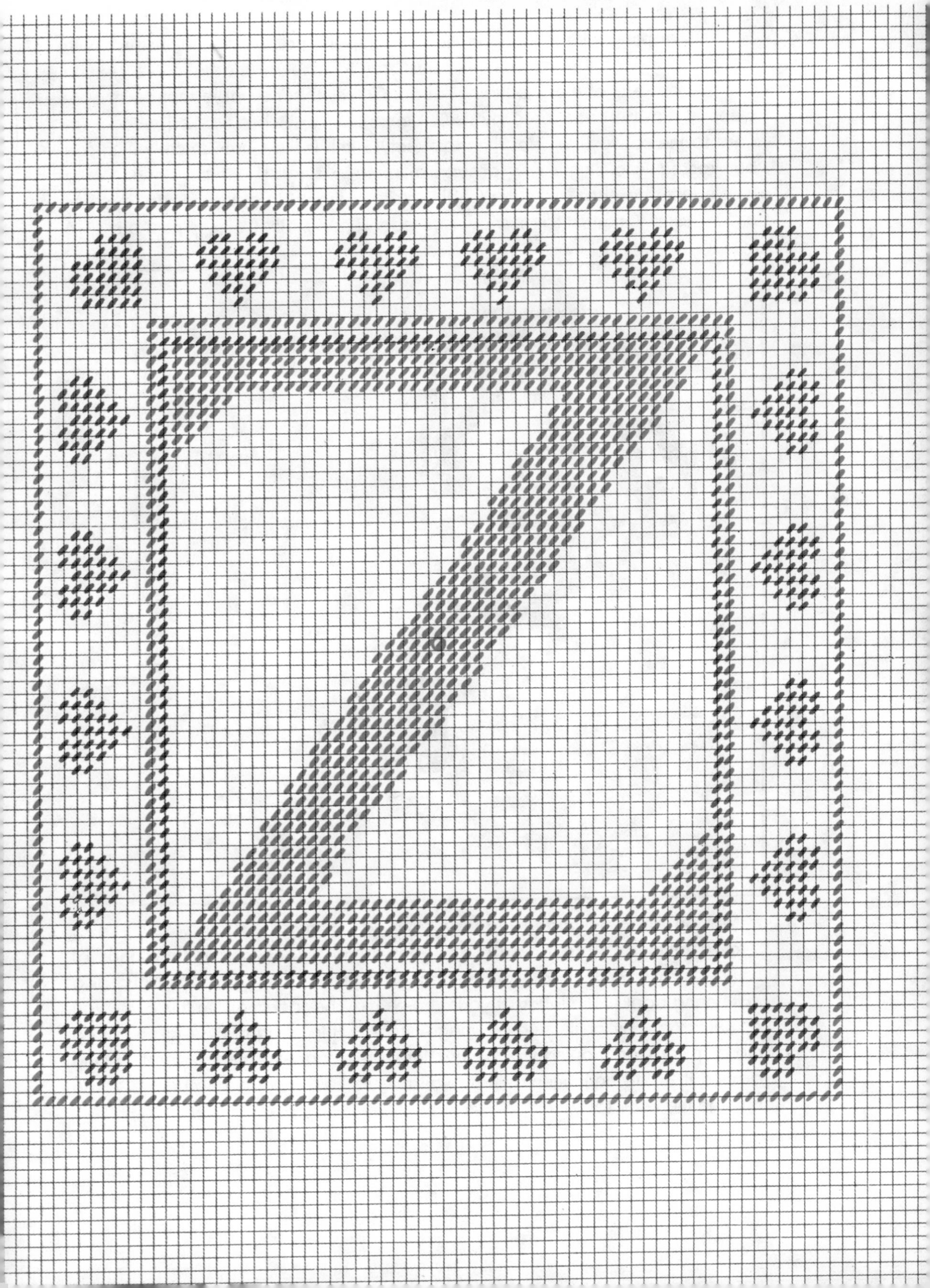

# HOW TO GRAPH LETTERS AND USE THEM IN NEEDLEPOINT

Stitchers working with lettering in their needlepoint are occasionally struck with the perversity of the canvas; you just can't make a smooth curve on the stepped off grid of the grounding fabric. Often, this inevitable feature of needlepoint can be conquered by use of embroidery stitches worked without regard to the canvas. Perhaps the most useful stitch is the Chain stitch, which can be worked in a single row around a letter to smooth out the curves, or a whole letter can be worked in Chain stitch off the grain of the canvas. A color picture using Chain stitch is shown on page ii, and other examples are shown here.

Moving on to uncharted territory, you may decide that you would like to stitch a letter or word from an alphabet found in one of the thousands of sources available to all of us in the masses of printed matter around and also in lettering books. The letter of your choice may be too small. In this case, you can enlarge it by projecting an image of the letter (using a slide taken with a close-up lens or slipping the picture into an opaque projector) and tracing around it. If this equipment is not available to you, have a photocopy house enlarge the letter for you.

It is worthwhile knowing that certain letters have similarities and should be kept as consistent as possible. E, F, H, I, L, and T are all composed of straight lines and are probably the easiest letters to work with (except in cursive styles). B, D, P, are R are related through a combination of straight lines and curves, and from these the O, C, Q, G, and U can be developed. J and S are odd-balls that have to be dealt with individually. V, W, Y, M, and N are related through straight and slanted lines. The A, K, X, and Z fit into this category but are difficult to work with when designing for needlepoint.

All letters in your "made up" alphabet should be the same height in upper case. The widths will vary. Lower-case letters have an average base height, but remember the b, d, h, l, f, and k have ascending strokes, and g, p, q, y, and j have descending strokes. It might be useful at this point to review some of the alphabets in this book, especially the Roman Magesty letters, to see how to go about stepping off the curves of all rounded letters to conform to the canvas grid. Extremely ornate or curvy letters are difficult to stitch and should be simplified. And graphing is a must. The authors have found that 10-ct. graph paper is the easiest size to work with. Some art supply stores have graph paper that is translucent. With this paper, a letter can be traced directly onto the graph paper, and refinements can be made from there. Otherwise, trace the letter onto tracing paper and tape this down on top of dime store graph paper. Your graphed version will be on the tracing paper, but you will be able to see through to the grid beneath. Remember to count carefully when setting up your letters. Draw a dotted block around the hand-drawn or reproduced letter on translucent graph paper or on tracing paper taped to dime store graph paper. This will establish the height and width of the area you are working with. To locate the center of your letter, count the height and width of the block and divide in half. Starting at the lower right corner, count midway across to the left and then count up halfway to find the middle. If the letter is an odd number of threads wide (e.g., 11), the center stitch will fall on the 6th thread. There will be 5 stitches to either side, and the letter will be squarely centered. If the letter is an even number of threads wide (e.g., 12), you should count across 6 threads and put your center over the 6th. The letter will be 1 stitch wider on one side than the other, but this is not noticeable. Then graph the letter stitch by stitch, conforming to the original lines as closely as possible. Many refinements and corrections can be made at this stage; however, actually stitching the letter is the only way to see the accuracy of your translation to needlepoint.

At this point, the mathematics of lettering for needlepoint may be getting you down or cramping your creative style. You can go back to the Chain stitch, or you can choose a huge, fairly intricate letter that is a design in itself and doesn't need counting out to the last stitch. The letters in illuminated manuscripts are particularly conducive to stitching, and while they often need simplifying before they can be worked, the decorations may suggest a variety of stitches that you use within the letter.

The Bibliography at the back of the book gives many sources of alphabets should you want to pursue "doing your own thing."

The Open sign is a combination of counted thread stitches, such as the Parisian background and the Basketweave flower and sun, and of more free-flowing embroidery stitches that are worked without regard to the canvas grid. The letters, all in Chain, appear smooth and without the stepped-off look that usually accompanies lettering on canvas.

The opposite side of the sign is just as effective, again using Chain stitch off the grid of the canvas to form the letters.

This beautiful letter is from the Second Bible of Charles the Bald, written, probably, in the eighth century. A large letter like this is a source of design inspiration for the needlepoint "penman." The dots surrounding the letter could be stitched in French Knots, and many of the stitches learned in a sampler class would be suitable for filling in the body of the letter. Remember when working with a highly ornate letter, such as this one, that some simplification will be necessary in the translation from written word to needlepointed word. A letter this large does not need to be diagramed. However, you will need to count out and diagram smaller letters found in the numerous sources of the written word that are available today.